A SERIES OF LESSONS IN ISLAM

Ethics

GOD, SOCIETY, AND ME

Sayyid Ali Al-Hakeem

THE MAINSTAY
FOUNDATION

Author: Sayyid Ali Al-Hakeem

Translated and Edited by: The Mainstay Foundation

Printed in the United States.

ISBN: 978-1943393879

To our guide. To our hope. To our salvation.

To our Prophet (s).

CONTENTS

ABOUT THE AUTHOR

Sayyid Ali Al-Hakeem is an esteemed Muslim scholar, lec-
turer, and researcher residing in Dubai, UAE. Sayyid Al-
Hakeem spent ten years studying at the Islamic seminaries
of Qum, Iran. There, he completed his Advanced Seminars
(a Ph.D. equivalent in Islamic seminaries) in Islamic Juris-
prudence and Thought. He also received a Master's degree
in Islamic Thought from the Islamic University of Lebanon.
Sayyid Al-Hakeem has dedicated the past twenty-two years
of his life to service of the Muslim community in different
capacities. He serves as a resident scholar in the Imam Has-
san Mosque, Dubai. He is the Chair of the Religious Committee and the religious supervisor of the Charitable Deeds
Committee of the Ja'afariya Endowment Charitable Council
of Dubai.

TRANSLATOR'S PREFACE

The task of translating Sayyid Ali Al-Hakeem's book was gratifying and enlightening. The book delivered precious nuggets of knowledge and polished pearls of wisdom in a style that is conversational and pleasant. This book is our attempt to pass these nuggets and pearls on to you in a style that is similarly conversational and pleasant. We thank the Sayyid for allowing us to benefit from this endeavor. We wish him a life filled with scholarly attainment in hopes that he will continue to pass along his treasures.

We must humbly however admit some of our biggest limitations in this endeavor. First, we must admit the great difficulty that comes with the attempting to translate the Holy Quran. Muslim scholars have pondered on the meanings of the holy text for centuries, and the meanings of its verses only grow deeper as time passes. The process of translation always begs us to find precise meanings for the passages that we translate. But when we encounter the majesty of the Holy Quran, we find ourselves incapable of understanding, let alone translating, its true and deep meanings. We turned to the works of translators who have attempted to do this before. Although no translation can do justice to the Holy Quran, we found that the translation of Ali Quri Qarai to be the most proper in understanding when compared to the understanding of the text as derived by our grand scholars. As such, we decided to rely on Qarai's translations throughout this book, with some adaptations that allowed us to weave the verses more properly with the rest of the work.

A second great limitation came with translation of the narrations of the Grand Prophet Muhammad (s) and his Holy Household (a). Their words are ever so deep and ever so powerful. We attempted to convey these passages to the reader in a tone that is understandable without deviating from the essence of the words of these immaculate personalities. We pray that we were successful in this endeavor.

Finally, we want to take this opportunity to thank you for your support. As students of Islam and as translators of this text, our greatest purpose is to please God by passing along these teachings to others. By picking up this book, you have lent your crucial support to this endeavor. We hope that you will continue your support throughout the rest of this book, and we ask that you keep us in prayers whenever you pick it up.

The Editorial and Translation Team,

The Mainstay Foundation

INTRODUCTION

In the name of God, the most Beneficent, the most Merciful

Praise be to God, Lord of the Worlds. May God send His peace and blessings to the most noble of His creatures, the Holy Prophet Muhammad (s) and his Holy Progeny (a).

This book, *Ethics: God, Society, and Me*, is a compilation of life lessons revolving around the moral character of a true Muslim. The focus and purpose of this work is to provide practical inspiration for the reader who is trying to lead a noble life in servicing God. With basic principles derived from the Holy Quran and the lives of the Prophet (s) and his Progeny (a), this book provides an overview of the Islamic code of ethics.

The teachings of Islam have one unequivocal goal – to allow its followers to pursue excellence. From that perspective, Islam places great emphasis on knowledge and learning. We can see this clearly in the verses of the Holy Quran. These verses give knowledge a special status that is unique when compared with other human virtues. God says in the Holy Quran, "*Say, 'Are those who know equal to those who do not know?' Only those who possess intellect take admonition."*[1] God also says, *"Only those of God's servants having knowledge fear Him."*[2]

The traditions of the Holy Prophet (s) and his Progeny (a) contain numerous similar admonitions as well. It is narrated that Imam Al-Sadiq (a) said, *"The Messenger of God (s) once said, 'Seeking knowledge is an obligation on every Muslim. Verily, God loves the seekers of knowledge.'"* It is also narrated that the Commander of the Faithful Ali ibn Abi Talib (a) once said,

> *Oh people! Know that excellence in faith consists of seeking knowledge and acting in accordance to that knowledge. Indeed, seeking knowledge is a higher obligation for you than seeking sustenance. Your sustenance is pre-ordained and guaranteed. Your Just Lord has divided it amongst you and promised to deliver it to you. Surely, He will keep His promise. [On the other hand,] knowledge is protected by its keepers. You were commanded to seek it from its keepers, so go forth and seek it.*

Islam did not stop at admonitions and theories about knowledge and learning. Instead, it created opportunities and enabled conditions that would foster learning, research, and study. Amongst these was the establishment of Friday prayers – God says in the Quran, *"O you who have faith! When the call is made for prayer on Friday, hurry toward the remembrance of God, and leave all business. That is better for you, should you know."*[3] One of the important pillars of this ritual is its sermon, where the prayer leader must convey Islam's teachings, in

---

[1] The Holy Quran. Chapter 39 [Arabic: *Al-Zumar*]. Verse 9.
[2] The Holy Quran. Chapter 35 [Arabic: *Fatir*]. Verse 28.
[3] The Holy Quran. Chapter 62 [Friday; Arabic: *Al-Jumaa*]. Verse 9.

addition to addressing all other relevant worldly and other-worldly matters.

Dear reader, this series of books is based on a compilation of Friday sermons that I delivered over the years, as well as lectures I gave at a number of commemorations and celebrations. Throughout such gatherings, I have been able to address and speak on a wide array of issues relevant to the Muslim community.

At the insistence of a number of dear brothers, I compiled my notes to write these books with the hopes that God will accept the work and that the benefit will spread to the believers. I tried to maintain the conversational tone of the original sermons in order to make the books more reader friendly. After a series of these books were originally printed in Arabic, a group of believers insisted on having the work translated into English so that English-speaking audiences may benefit as well.

I thank God, the Exalted, for His infinite support and favor. I must also thank everyone who participated in making this book a reality.

I ask God, the Almighty, to take this work as an act of devotion for His sake and to accept it by His grace, He is surely the All-Kind and Magnanimous.

Ali Al-Hakeem,

Dubai, United Arab Emirates

HEEDLESSNESS

In the name of God, the most Beneficent, the most Merciful

[A]nd the true promise draws near [to its fulfillment], behold, the faithless will look on with a fixed gaze: 'Woe to us! We have certainly been oblivious of this! Indeed, we have been wrongdoers!'[1]

This verse speaks of the fate of those who disbelieved in God and the reality in which they will find themselves. Unbelievers here are those who have preoccupied themselves with matters other than the afterlife, clinging on to the worldly life and all its glitter. They have worked tirelessly to stay here in a desire of being somewhat eternal, without paying attention to the fact that there is another life that they will inevitably face. Thus, when the promise of truth that God ensures does come, the human being who has been blinded by the worldly life will stand confused and even shocked. He will stand eyes wide open, unable to blink, as he sees the punishment of God prepared for those who have went against His will and turned to sin. Thus, they find themselves in a realized state of woe, despair, and

---

[1] The Holy Quran. Chapter 21 [The Prophets; Arabic: *Al-Anbiyya*]. Verse 97.

grief, because they were heedless to the consequences that they are about to experience.

Moreover, the verse discusses a dangerous disease which affects us as humans in this life, and though we may not realize it, its affects are shown in the afterlife. This disease strikes the soul of the human and disallows him from reaching the path of God. This disease is what the Quran describes as heedlessness. It is significant to discuss and understand this topic and to realize both its causes and effects. Realizing the reasons for heedlessness and its signs, one can work to prevent it and thus be free of its shackles. To free oneself from heedlessness is to enjoy true happiness both in this world and the next.

This discussion is comprised of a number of key points:

DESTINED FOR PARADISE

The All-wise God created human beings with the goal of giving them the opportunity to end up in a paradise even more distinct than the one where they started. For paradise and everything in it was created for the human, and it is a place established for them to enjoy its pleasures and benefits while serving and worshiping God. When our forefather Adam made the choice to begin his difficult test on earth, he departed the initial paradise and descended to a realm where an ultimate paradise had to be earned through trials and tribulations. The dynamics of the earthly examination meant that one's transgressions and sins could prevent him/her from entering paradise. Just like a person who is justifiably prevented entry to a safe zone for having a vile virus, a person who carries sin can be rightfully prevented entry into paradise.

> *We said, 'Get down from it, all together! Yet, should any guidance come to you from Me, those who follow My guidance shall have no fear, nor shall they grieve. But those who are faithless and deny Our signs, they shall be the inmates of the Fire and they shall remain in it [forever].*[2]

WE HAVE A PURPOSE

God created the human in this world to test and try him. And this life will end when Judgement Day comes and humans will be given the balance of their deeds, good for good and bad for bad: *"Blessed is He in whose hands is all sovereignty, and He has power over all things. He, who created death and life that He may test you [to see] which of you is best in conduct. And He is the All-mighty, the All-forgiving."*[3] If there was not a Day where God would reward the righteous and punish the corrupter – a meaningful end to the trials of this world – then the whole work of creation would be in vain. But God, the Wise, does nothing in vain. What would be the benefit for a person to do good in this world and prohibit himself from so many desires and pleasures, if life is only a limited number of years that end in utter nonexistence. If it were not for resurrection and the promise by God to bring humanity forth toward Judgment, humanity's movement towards God would stop. The believer and the unbeliever, the obedient and the disobedient, would all be in the same position with-

---

[2] The Holy Quran. Chapter 2 [The Cow; Arabic: *Al-Baqara*]. Verses 38 and 39.

[3] The Holy Quran. Chapter 67 [The Dominion; Arabic: *Al-Mulk*] Verses 1 and 2.

out any distinction. There would be no meaning for sacrifice, or for standing up against and taming one's carnal desires. This world would become a jungle where no two would be able to agree to even a single idea or opinion. Chaos alone would emerge as people would hurt and kill one another for nothing but self-satisfaction.

DIVINE LAW

If we know this, then we also know there is no doubt that God would deliver a law to protect humanity. There must be a system of law that cares for humanity throughout its journey on the path that God wanted for it. God created humanity and sent people prophets and messengers to teach, warn, protect and guide all towards Him. God did this so people would not fall to their whims and follow Satan, and moreover, as part of His divine wisdom in monitoring and protecting His creation.

> *With Him are the treasures of the Unseen; no one knows them except Him. He knows whatever there is in land and sea. No leaf falls without His knowing it, nor is there a grain in the darkness of the earth, nor anything fresh or withered but it is in a manifest Book.[4]*

God Also says:

> *On that day, mankind will issue forth in various groups to be shown their deeds. So whoever does an atom's weight of good will see it, and whoever does an atom's weight of evil will see it.[5]*

---

[4] The Holy Quran. Chapter 6 [The Cattle; Arabic: *Al-An'am*]. Verse 59.
[5] The Holy Quran. Chapter 99[The Quake; Arabic: *Al-Zalzala*]. Verses 6-8.

Divine monitoring prevents humanity from completely leaving the righteous path and helps people in their behavior and course towards God. However, when the heart is met with veils caused by the practice of sin, that person is like someone who is walking a path with several hurdles while blindfolded. He cannot see and he is bound to trip over those obstacles. On the other hand, the person who keeps his eyes open will definitely avoid a lot of those obstacles and manage to walk down that path more easiely. In the same way, the person who chooses to stay in a state of remembrance and reminding oneself of God will take himself closer to his own perfection and completion.

A SPIRITUAL DISEASE

Heedlessness is the self being lazy and sluggish to paying attention to its responsibilities and duties. A person who is heedless could know what is best for him, but for one reason or another, he creates veils or barriers between his heart that calls him towards doing good and his acknowledgement of the path of good. And thus, he lives in a maze bouncing from wall to wall, not knowing which course to take and how to conduct himself. Unfortunately, he doesn't realize this until he is shocked with the reality of death – a promise of truth by God – that leads him to feel the oppression he caused in his relationship with God.

For this reason, the believer should be wary about this spiritual disease that could really blind him. In the same manner that a person would want to protect his vision and eyesight, he should consider even more maintaining his insight. This emphasis on protecting one's insight is due to the fact that the effects of heedlessness are even more detrimental to a person than that of being blind. A blind person can go about this life and adapt in one way or another to live effectively in this world. But can a heedless person adapt to hellfire, as he is unable to describe it or even acknowledge its essence? Imam Al-Sadiq (a) warns us about heedlessness in the following narration: *"Beware of heedlessness. Whoever is heedless, neglects his own self. Beware of taking God for granted. Whoever takes God for granted, God will dishonor him on the Day of Judgment."*[6]

THE REASONS BEHIND IT

Realizing the meaning of heedlessness we must progress further to learn the reasons behind it. The following issues are key to understanding the reasons for this disease, as derived from our understanding of the Quranic verses and the noble narrations.

Oppression

Oppression is characteristic of mankind. But people do not stop at oppressing one another, but rather, they go on to oppress themselves. And the greatest oppression is when mankind chooses oppression in his relationship with God. This happens when a person is showered with the blessings of life and responds to those blessings with wrongdoing and disbelief. And thus, the greatest oppression is associating a partner with God. This is evidenced by the words of Luqman as told in the Holy Quran, *"When Luqman said to his*

---

[6] Al-Barqi, *Al-Mahasin*, 96.

son, as he advised him: O my son! Do not ascribe any partners to God. Polytheism is indeed a great injustice."[7]

And from here we observe that one of the causes of heedlessness is oppression. The following verse describes this from the perspective of those who are heedless: *"Woe to us! We have certainly been oblivious of this! Indeed, we have been wrongdoers!*"[8] Allamah Tabatabaei explains this verse in his Exegesis — Tafsir Al-Mizan. This refers to the words of the unbelievers when they witnessed the 'hour,' they stood with grief and woe. They admitted to their heedlessness as an effect of the oppression in which they partook by busying themselves with things that made them forget the afterlife. For that they said, in reference to themselves, *"we were wrongdoers."*[9] [10]

Befriending people who are wicked and wanton

There is no doubt that befriending wicked and wanton individuals is one of the causes of veiling the heart and inducing heedlessness. Wicked people tend to prettify their misdeeds to others as to attract others to join them. A person who is wicked or wanton does not find comfort until he finds others to participate and partner with him in wrongdoing. Befriending people who are heedless is a cause for heedlessness, and thus we see God warning the believers about this sort of friendship in the following verse:

> *Content yourself with the company of those who supplicate their Lord morning and evening, desiring His Face, and do not lose sight of them, desiring the glitter of the life of this*

---

[7] The Holy Quran. Chapter 31 [Arabic: *Luqman*]. Verse 13.
[8] The Holy Quran. Chapter 21 [The Prophets; Arabic: *Al-Anbiyya*]. Verse 97.
[9] Ibid.
[10] Al-Tabatabaei, *Tafsir Al-Mizan*, 14:327.

world. And do not obey him whose heart We have made oblivious to Our remembrance, and who follows his own desires, and whose conduct is [mere] profligacy. [11]

When a person befriends such people, he will undoubtedly experience a state of regret on the Day of Judgment. God said: *"It will be a day when the wrongdoer will bite his hands, saying: I wish I had followed the Apostle's way! Woe to me! I wish I had not taken so and so as a friend!"*[12]

This verse indicates an important reality, that befriending heedless people results in heedlessness. That friendship is realized with regret and guilt on the Day of Judgment, as people stand wishing they had never had those relationships that have caused such regret.

Not Praying

One of the causes of heedlessness is not praying. Prayer is the remembrance of God. This prayer is a practical exercise for people to remember Him at least five times throughout the day. If a person truly practices and upholds his prayer, there is no doubt that he will protect himself from the disease of heedlessness – a disease that kills the heart and blinds one's insight. Imam Al-Hassan (a) describes heedlessness as the following: *"Heedlessness is your abandoning of the mosque and your obedience to the corrupt."*[13]

This truth is also realized from the words of Imam Al-Baqir (a) when he says, *"The believer who upholds his obligatory prayers,*

---

[11] The Holy Quran. Chapter 18 [The Cave; Arabic: *Al-Kahf*]. Verse 28.

[12] The Holy Quran. Chapter 25 [Arabic: *Al-Furqan*]. Verses 27-28.

[13] Al-Majlisi, *Bihar Al-Anwar*, 75:115.

and prays them on time, is not of the heedless."[14] Prayer has a great effect on the presence of heedlessness. Leaving prayer mandates heedlessness, while upholding prayer mandates protection from heedlessness.

Indulgence in the Love of the World

There is no doubt that indulging in the love of this worldly life and following one's carnal desires causes one to have a barrier with God. It is impossible to combine the love of God and the love of the worldly life in the heart of a believer. A person who makes this world his biggest concern and the extent of his seeking does not think about anything but that. Because he is so preoccupied, he is unable to free himself to even think of his captive state. Thus, he becomes heedless of God and what God has prepared for His righteous followers:

> *Indeed those who do not expect to encounter Us and who are pleased with the life of this world and satisfied with it, and those who are oblivious of Our signs – it is they whose refuge shall be the Fire because of what they used to earn. Indeed those who have faith and do righteous deeds, their Lord guides them by the means of their faith. Streams will run for them in gardens of bliss.*[15]

This world, in a way, becomes a prison for some people. They do not seek meeting with God because they have sold themselves into slavery to the world and do not wish to escape and free themselves. They do not see it as enslavement though, they see it as bliss, and because of that they do not

---

[14] Al-Kulayni, *Al-Kafi*, 3:270.
[15] The Holy Quran. Chapter 10 [Jonah; Arabic: *Younus*]. Verses 7-9.

wish to escape. Thus, heedlessness is actuated and in it they remain.

The aforementioned four points are the most significant causes for heedlessness and the reason fora person to become neglectful of God and his relationship with Him.

HEARTS, EARS, AND EYES

The heedless is one who lives in veils and darkness whereby he cannot find the light to guide his way. Nor can he see a world that is bigger and more welcoming than the one where he already lives. In the following verse, God describes this person with several attributes:

> *Certainly We have winnowed out for hell many of the jinn and humans: they have hearts with which they do not understand, they have eyes with which they do not see, they have ears with which they do not hear. They are like cattle; indeed, they are more astray. It is they who are the heedless.*[16]

Every human being has a heart, ears, and eyes, but not every person benefits from these tools. If a person goes on without utilizing these tools in their intended manner, it would be no different if those tools were present or not. The heart was created to understand the signs of God and to be the vessel of holy truths. However, when the heart is veiled from such signs and truths, then that heart is robbed from its intended benefit. The eyes were created to ease mankind's journey through life, to gaze upon the signs of God as a clear connected path toward God, and to understand godly truths. But if a person were to use his eyes for things

---

[16] The Holy Quran. Chapter 7 [The Heights; Arabic: *Al-Aaraf*]. Verse 179.

other than obedience to God, then the existence or inexistence of those eyes would be the same. Rather, those eyes being inexistent would be better for that person as to not indulge in sin and heedlessness through one of God's blessings. In the same way, God created for us ears to listen to His signs and the beneficial truths for this life and the next.

These are the most significant characteristics with which to describe a heedless person, as mentioned by God in the Holy Quran. In addition, these characteristics can be observed in the situations we have previously mentioned as the causes for heedlessness: neglecting prayer or taking it for granted, befriending wicked and wanton people, and being indulgent in this world and its pleasures.

It is important to note that it is possible for a person who is a believer to fall into some of these mistakes as a result of being in a temporary state of heedlessness. The heedlessness that we have previously discussed, as evidenced by the Quranic verses and the noble narrations, is in reference to the person who has been overcome by those mentioned causes and has made heedlessness his default state. Thus, it is imperative for the believer who falls into some of these situations to pull himself back and protect himself from falling further into heedlessness. If he does not work to protect himself, before he knows it he can be in so deep that he cannot escape from heedlessness and its shackles.

Obedience and disobedience to God are the measure of remembrance versus heedlessness. The Holy Prophet (s) is narrated to have said,

> *Whoever is obedient to God is one who remembered Him, even if he has lessened [the number of] his prayers, fasts,*

and recitations of the Holy Quran. And whoever is disobedient to God is one who is heedless of Him, even if he has increased [the number of] his prayers, fasts, and recitations of the Holy Quran.[17]

In this discussion Allamah Tabatabaei notes:

... Disobedience of the servant does not take place except by heedlessness and forgetfulness. If a person were to remember the reality of his disobedience and its effects, he would not go forward with such wrongdoing. This is unless that person is one who is not concerned about disobeying, even when reminded of God, and does not care about the status of his Lord. This type of person is simply tyrannical and ignorant of the status of God, the highness of His glory, and the extent of His reach.[18]

DEADLY EFFECTS

There is no doubt that heedlessness has effects that result in punishment by God to the heedless, amongst them are:

The Death of the Heart

The heart is the spring of a person's life. One's humanity is not complete except by the life of that heart. The heart that is alive is a pointer to the life of the human being. Likewise, the heart that is dead is a pointer to the death of that human being. This is regardless of whether that person is inhaling and exhaling. For a person who has a dead heart is one whose existence or nonexistence are the same; and heedlessness is the cause to the death of the heart. The Com-

---

[17] Al-Saduq, *Ma'ani Al-Akhbar*, 399.

[18] Al-Tabatabaei, *Tafsir Al-Mizan*, 1:342.

mander of the Faithful, Imam Ali (a), said: *"Whoever has been overcome by heedlessness, his heart has died."*[19] Staying in a state of heedlessness, however, causes the death of the heart after going through a number of stages. Those stages include the hardening of the heart and the blinding of one's insight.

Imam Al-Baqir (a) connects the relationship between heedlessness and hardening of the heart when he says: *"Beware of heedlessness, for in it exists the hardening of the heart."*[20] Regarding the blinding of one's insight, Imam Ali (a) says: *"Staying in heedlessness blinds the insight."*[21] And from this we see the great effects of heedlessness on the heart of the human being. The mentioned narrations concur with the following Quranic verse: *"they have hearts with which they do not understand…"*[22]

Going Astray

There is no doubt that the person who lives in a state of heedlessness also lives in a state of vanity, deviation, and becoming farther from God. The heart cannot see the light of guidance while it is veiled from God. Such a heart is far away from the remembrance of God and the remembrance of His verses and teachings. It is not possible for such a heart to become a station for divine light, for such a heart lives in the darkness of heedlessness. Whoever is like this, there is no doubt that he is on a path of deviation and dis-

---

[19] Al-Wasiti, *'Uyoon Al-Hikam wa Al-Mawa'ez*, 504.
[20] Al-Harrani, *Tohaf Al-'Oqool*, 285.
[21] Al-Wasiti, *'Uyoon Al-Hikam wa Al-Mawa'ez*, 250.
[22] The Holy Quran. Chapter 7 [The Heights; Arabic: *Al-Aaraf*]. Verse 179.

tance from God. This is what Imam Ali (a) illustrates for us in his saying: *"There is enough deviation in heedlessness."*[23]

All in all, there are many negative effects from heedlessness. These include but are not limited to corruption, vanity, arrogance, and other destructive characteristics and habits.

---

[23] Al-Wasiti, *'Uyoon Al-Hikam wa Al-Mawa'ez,* 385.

SPIRITUAL SUSTENANCE

In the name of God, the most Beneficent, the most Merciful

Indeed We created man from the drop of a mixed fluid so that We may put him to the test, so We endowed with hearing and sight. Indeed We have guided him to the way, be he grateful or ungrateful.[1]

BODY AND SOUL

God (SWT) created mankind in the best of forms and honored him over all other creations; so much so that mankind was given the position of deputy[2] over all creation. God created mankind with two components: the physical body and the "soul" or the "self." These two components are connected and interdependent in this world. For the duration of our existence in this world, the two remain connected. They are not separated until the moment of death, when the body is worn by death and the soul begins its transition.

---

[1] The Holy Quran, Chapter 76 [Man; Arabic: *Al-Insan*], Verses 2 and 3.

[2] Arabic: *Khalifa.*

What Makes Us Human

One might ask, "which of the two components is more important? The body or the soul? Is the physical being what makes us human? Or is it the eternal soul that is essential to humanity?"

If we look into the Holy Quran, we will find that humanity is realized through the soul, or the self. It is that component that has consciousness, harbors a will, and drives human action. And although the soul and the self take action through the physical body, that physical body is only a tool for the soul to interact with the physical world. And so we find that verses that speak to the issue of guidance and misguidance are addressed to the self. God says in His Holy Book *"By the soul and Him who fashioned it, and inspired it with [discernment between] its virtues and vices."*[3]

Such verses are addressed to the soul and not to the body, and that is because the body is in a state of constant change. Nature is always taking its toll on the body. A person who has just been born is very different in ten years,. very different at twenty years, and again very different at eighty. The body is in a state of constant physiological change. And so all characteristics and titles that we address to a person are addressed to the soul and the self. This self is the principal and the body is only an extension and a tool for it. God (SWT) says:

> *"Certainly We created man from an extract of clay. Then We made him a drop of [seminal] fluid [lodged] in a secure abode. Then We created the drop of fluid as a clinging*

---

[3] The Holy Quran, Chapter 91 [The Sun; Arabic: *Al-Shams*], Verses 7 and 8.

mass. Then We created the clinging mass as a fleshy tissue. Then We created the fleshy tissue as bones. Then We clothed the bones with flesh. Then We produced him as [yet] another creature. So blessed is God, the best of creators! Then indeed you die after that. Then you will indeed be raised up on the Day of Resurrection."[4]

And so we see that the soul is the stronger component of an individual's being, the dimension which remains constant throughout all the physical changes. Indeed, we can even say that the soul is trapped in a prison that is the body, and is only freed from this prison at death. And at that point, some blessed souls will be called out: *"O soul at peace! Return to your Lord, pleased and pleasing! Then enter among My servants, and enter My paradise!"*[5]

From this perspective, we must realize that nourishment of the spiritual aspect of an individual is much more important than any physical or bodily nourishment. Yet because we live in a material state and can feel it all around us wherever we turn, we become forgetful of this truth and start prizing the physical world and our physical bodies rather than giving the necessary care and nourishment to the more important aspect of our being.

APPRECIATION OF SPIRITUALITY

The soul has a power that surpasses the power of the body. The soul is what drives the body and all actions are determined by the soul before they are undertaken by the body.

---

[4] The Holy Quran, Chapter 23 [The Believers; Arabic: *Al-Muminoon*], Verses 12-16.
[5] The Holy Quran, Chapter 89 [The Dawn; Arabic: *Al-Fajr*], Verses 27-30.

The soul is a metaphysical and simple being, yet it holds potentials that the body does not. The soul can launch into a greater universe and can perceive many things that cannot be seen by the body. A vision that a person may have is a perception of the soul of worlds that cannot be reached by the body. So you see that a person might be asleep in his own bed, but can see events occurring in places that are thousands of miles away, or events that have occurred in the past or ones that are to occur in the future. All this is because of the specific properties of the soul. Imam Sadiq (a) was asked by Abu Basir: "A man or a woman might be asleep but they see that they are in Mecca or in another land. Are their souls outside of their bodies?" The Imam replied "*No, Abu Basir. If the soul was to depart the body, it will not return to it. Rather it is like the sun; its location is in the sky, but its rays are throughout this world.*"[6] And this tells us that the soul has the ability to encompass and transcend the time and place of the physical body.

From this perspective, any intelligent individual would give greater emphasis to the spiritual aspect than on the physical aspect of his or her being. And although the physical aspect of being has its rights and must be appreciated in itself, it does not mean that it can overshadow the more important spiritual aspect. When a person is hungry, he must find a way to fulfill his hunger; but that source of fulfillment must not have a negative effect on his soul. Forbidden or Haram food would add to the oppression of the self and would create barriers to the transcendence of the soul. And so we also see, for example, that when a person needs to fulfill his

---

[6] Al-Majlisi, *Bihar Al-Anwar*, 58:43.

sexual desires, he must take into account the consequences that may affect the soul. A person cannot fulfill his desires through impermissible means and be heedless of the potential effects on the soul. An impermissible look, fornication, or an impermissible touch; these are all actions that lead the soul into a world of darkness that stifles its growth.

THE BENEFITS OF SPIRITUALITY

Once we understand the importance of the spiritual aspect of our being and the role of the soul in a human's worldly and other-worldly life, we see that appreciation of this aspect has a number of benefits. If we appreciate the self and purify it, our ability to understand the truth and discover hidden meanings will be greater; as the eye of insight that is associated with the self will be able to see much more than the physical eye. If there is a veil covering the eye of insight, we may not be able to understand the truth and ultimately reach knowledge of God – that knowledge that would allow us to reach the paradise of Heaven. And whenever a person disregards the soul in fulfilling the needs of the body, the imprisonment of the soul will become harsher – minimizing the ability of the individual to reach the high potentials of the soul that could ultimately lead to happiness in both worlds. An individual who is guided by insight and is blessed with a clear vision will not be entrenched in this world, and his path toward God will be easy and clear. And this is the benefit of taking care of the spiritual aspect of our being, refining it, and training it well.

THE MEANS TO SPIRITUAL SUSTENANCE

One may ask "how can an individual go about spiritual nourishment – especially with the many claims that are circulated about this issue – in a correct way that would lead to the greatest growth for the soul?"

Before we tackle this issue, we must mention that attention to issues of spirituality is not something which is restricted to Muslims alone. Most religions give special emphasis to spirituality. In Hinduism, for example, we see a method of extreme exercises that lead to some form of transcendence of the soul. Those who practice these exercises attain knowledge of some truths and begin teaching about them. We see them giving treatments to some illnesses. Modern science stresses that there are a large number of illnesses that stem from the soul. We may look at those who partake in these spiritual exercises and find that what they do is beyond the bounds of nature. But that is because of our own spiritual weakness. In truth, these abilities are accessible to those who partake in these special exercises. And we see this with priests in a number of other religions who are able to use their spirituality to cure some illnesses. And those abilities are used by each religion to call people towards it and for proselytization purposes.

The truth of the matter is that these spiritual exercises or any system of subjugating the body and controlling the whims and desires will lead to such abilities. And this may be taken advantage of, even in satanic ways. These spiritual effects do not mean that the individual is walking on the path of God, as these abilities are inherent in the laws and balances of nature. Any form of the subjugation of the desires will lead to transcendence of the self. But is this the right form of transcendence? Is this freedom that is granted to the soul the correct type of freedom? In other words, is this type of struggle pleasing to God?

Islam provides us with a philosophy that is different from all the others. We see a number of distinguishing factors in our faith, the most important of which are as follows:

Firstly, Islam does not look at subjugation of the desires and self-purification as ways to reach the limited goal of obtaining a number of abilities. Rather, self-purification in accordance with Islamic teachings is a means to reach closeness to God and to attain His pleasure. Yes, a person might obtain such abilities on his journey towards God, but they are not the goal. Obtaining such abilities or not obtaining them makes no difference where it matters. Seeking closeness to God is our principal purpose. Closeness to God is measured by the extent of one's obedience to God. Spiritual powers have no bearing in that regard.

Secondly, this allows us to see that Islamic teachings are comprehensive in all regards. Our teachings place an emphasis on the spiritual aspect of life as well as on the physical aspect. Our religion does not teach us that self-purification comes from the subjugation of the body through actions such as refraining of marriage (i.e. celibacy) or renouncing all worldly pleasures (i.e. monasticism). Even worship has its own system, process, and times. God says *"We did not send down to you the Quran that you should be miserable."*[7] The body has its rights, as does the soul. This creates a

---

[7] The Holy Quran, Chapter 20 [Arabic: *Ta-Ha*], Verse 2.

complete balance between the material and the metaphysical needs of the individual.

Thirdly, we see that Islam creates a link between knowledge and education and spiritual nourishment. Spiritual nourishment must coincide with knowledge and learning. That is why we see that the people who are closest to self-purification and spirituality are our scholars who are well-learned in the religion. As for those who claim to have such abilities without the requisite knowledge, they have a great chance of falling into error or turning these acts of spiritual nourishment into simplistic rituals without realization of their meaning.

And so we can say that the process of self-purification in Islam is one of worship and a relationship with God. It is a process of awareness and not a process of ignorance. This allows us to understand the meaning of some of the narrations that declare "*the reflection of an hour is greater than the worship of a full year*,"[8] or "*the death of a scholar is more joyous to Satan than the death of seventy worshippers*,"[9] and similar narrations. So what value does worship have if it is not built on a sound basis of religious knowledge?

---

[8] Ibn Babaweih, *Fiqh Al-Rida*, 380.
[9] Ibn Al-Sabbagh, *Al-Fusool Al-Muhimma fi Marifa Al-Aimma*, 2:887.

FAITH

In the name of God, the most Beneficent, the most Merciful

Is he who founds his building on Godwariness and [the pursuit of God's] pleasure better-off or he who founds his building on the brink of a collapsing bank which collapses with him into the fire of hell? God does not guide the wrongdoing lot.[1]

No Two people will disagree with the fact that the fundamental element for any modern community is ethics. Nations and communities advance through the establishment of ethics. The more formidable the principles of ethics are in a community, the more those principles will harness the potential in that society to advance and make gains for it. Likewise, when such principles are weakened, there is more reason to see division and destruction in that very same society. If we look back in history, we see that the reason for the decline and fall of certain empires or societies was due to their decline in ethics and morals. It is true that some communities may survive such a decline, but those communities will have a weakened foundation. Eventually that

---

[1] The Holy Quran. Chapter 9 [The Repentance; Arabic: *Al-Tawba*] Verse 109.

weak foundation will give out and that community will fall. This is a divine order to which the Holy Quran points in a number of verses when mentioning nations or communities that have fallen. God said,

> *Have they not travelled through the land so that they may observe how was the fate of those who were before them? They were greater than them in might and with respect to the effects [they left] in the land. But then God seized them for their sins, and they had no defender against God['s punishment].*[2]

Other verses point to similar examples of the fall and punishment of such communities due to their moral decay. God speaks of the punishment descended upon the people of Lot for their sexual deviation in the following verse: *"Then We poured down upon them a rain [of stones]. So observe how was the fate of the guilty!"*[3]

Punishment was sent down on the people of Madyan for their deviation and corruption in economic transactions. Cheating the system and not being truthful to the scales of weighing products were reasons for God's punishment. *"So the earthquake seized them, and they lay lifeless prostrate in their homes."*[4]

And this is the case with other nations – decay in ethics and morals results in the fall of that nation or community. God said,

---

[2] The Holy Quran. Chapter 40 [The Forgiver; Arabic: *Ghafir*] Verse 21.
[3] The Holy Quran. Chapter 7 [The Heights; Arabic: *Al-Aaraf*]. Verse 84.
[4] Ibid. Verse 91.

And when We desire to destroy a town We command its af-
fluent ones [to obey God]. But they commit transgression in
it, and so the word becomes due against it, and We destroy
it utterly. How many generations We have destroyed since
Noah! Your Lord is sufficient as [a witness who is] well
aware and percipient of His servants' sins.[5]

In this discussion, we tie the role of faith to building the foundational code of ethics. In addition, we will discuss the fundamental difference between the vision of faith in regards to ethics and other perspectives on ethics. There are two fundamental points in discussing the rules and foundation on which ethics are built on in the scope of faith: the role of faith in building the foundation of ethics, and the ethical foundations and support system in the vision or lens of faith.

THE ROLE OF FAITH IN THE FOUNDATION OF ETHICS

Perhaps the words of the Holy Prophet (s) telling his people that, "*I was sent to perfect the best of ethics,*" summarize much of this discussion for us. The Holy Prophet (s) made evident that the most fundamental goal of his prophet-hood was to establish the best of ethics possible through the rules and laws he will relay and execute. This in fact is the fundamental goal of every prophet who came. On this premise, we see that faith is a fundamental pillar of ethics. Every virtue you can possibly think of – justice, generosity, nobility, honor, etc. – are all founded in faith. Faith is the root of such vir-

---

[5] The Holy Quran. Chapter 17 [The Ascension; Arabic: *Al-Israa*]. Verses 16-17.

tues and ethics. This is due to the fact that faith focuses on taming the self, monitoring one's behavior, controlling one's desires and whims, and restricting certain pleasures. All of these are fundamental rules of ethics. Ethics is manifested when these things are established. When one's selfishness is restricted, ethics is able to come to fruition. Likewise, generosity spreads through society when selflessness and altruism take the place of greed and self-interest. This is the case with many other virtues as well; sacrifice of something materialistic is usually the factor upon which virtue is contingent.

Nonetheless, there needs to be an incentive for a person to make such sacrifices and for such virtue to be established in the scope of ethics. If there was not an incentive then why would a person let go of what is within his reach and what would bring him happiness and pleasure? Would someone spend a great deal of money on something that is of very little worth? So how is it that it is expected for one to prohibit himself from so many material things without having something of great value in return? We cannot imagine anyone or anything able to compensate people for sacrificing in these matters other than God himself. This is understood through both the material and moral support given to us by Him in exchange for the sacrifices we make. The following verses illustrate this point:

> *The parable of those who spend their wealth in the way of God is that of a grain which grows seven ears, in every ear a hundred grains. God enhances severalfold whomever He wishes, and God is all-bounteous, all-knowing.*[6]

---

[6] The Holy Quran. Chapter 2 [The Cow; Arabic: *Al-Baqara*]. Verse 261.

What God gives is much greater than what we sacrifice.

"Spend in the way of God, and do not cast yourselves with your own hands into destruction; and be virtuous. Indeed God loves the virtuous."[7] The reward or compensation here cannot be ascertained through a monetary value because the love of God does not have a price tag. The love and favor of God is greater than anything and everything, because through that love a person can attain everything.

> *The love of [worldly] allures, including women and children, accumulated piles of gold and silver, horses of mark, livestock, and farms has been made to seem decorous to mankind. Those are the wares of the life of this world, but the goodness of one's ultimate destination lies near God. Say, 'Shall I inform you of something better than that? For those who are Godwary there will be gardens near their Lord, with streams running in them, to remain in them [forever], and chaste mates, and God's pleasure.' And God watches His servants. Those who say, 'Our Lord! Indeed, we have faith. So forgive us our sins, and save us from the punishment of the Fire.' [They are] patient and truthful, obedient and charitable, and they plead for [God's] forgiveness at dawns.*[8]

This verse points to the fact that people desire material things, as such things have been made appealing to them, and people work to attain those material things in satisfying their desires. The verse continues to show the limitation of self-satisfaction and warning the individual of the presence

---

[7] Ibid. Verse 195.
[8] The Holy Quran. Chapter 3 [Arabic: *Aal Imran*]. Verses 14-17.

of something greater than material gain. The path to attaining these blessings is practicing the best of ethics. This is evidenced by God's words in describing those who are influenced by what God has for them, over what this world has to offer, as those who have the best of virtues in patience, honesty, spending righteously, in addition to submitting to God's will through supplication and repentance.

Thus, the role of faith is clear in the establishment of the fundamental rules upon which ethics are built. Faith limits the love of one's self that misleads, controls and disobeys – for that disobedience is characteristic of that self, "*Indeed man becomes rebellious when he considers himself without need.*"[9] The great reward and compensation that a person can receive from sacrificing some materialistic things, by way of holding on to his ethics, can only be brought forth by God. For God is the one who knows the affairs of the individual, public and private, what is in his best interest, and what goes on in his mind – God is aware of all of it.

ETHICAL PRINCIPLES

There are a number of fundamental elements upon which ethics are built for both the individual and society as a whole. The most important of these elements are: **devotion to God, impartiality in moral conduct,** and **ethics as a complete system.**

---

[9] The Holy Quran. Chapter 96 [The Clot; Arabic: *Al-Alaq*]. Verses 6-7.

Devotion to God

Faith entrenches the understanding and formidable foundation of devotion to God as a prerequisite to any successful activity or endeavor, especially moral conduct and ethics. The societies that hold the features of ethical completeness are ones soundly built on the correct foundation.

> *Is he who founds his building on Godwariness and [the pursuit of God's] pleasure better-off or he who founds his building on the brink of a collapsing bank which collapses with him into the fire of hell? God does not guide the wrongdoing lot.*[10]

There is no doubt that a person's deepest honesty stems from his love and devotion to God. Likewise, a person's justice, goodness, honor, generosity, and all other virtues stem most naturally from the person's desire to please God out of love and dedication. "*Piety is [personified by] those who… give their wealth, for the love of Him, to relatives, orphans, the needy, the traveler and the beggar, and for [the freeing of] the slaves….*"[11]

However, if a person's motives and intentions are not for God, then his foundations are weak and everything he builds on these foundations will fall and result in the person's own collapse. His collapse is not merely figurative, for he will actually collapse into hellfire. This is because he chose to build a foundation that was other than devotion to God – and such a foundation is weak and bound to fall apart. God draws a comparison between this and the 'House of a Spider' in the following verse:

---

[10] The Holy Quran. Chapter 9 [The Repentance; Arabic: *Al-Tawba*]. Verse 109
[11] The Holy Quran. Chapter 2 [The Cow; Arabic: *Al-Baqara*]. Verse 177

The parable of those who take guardians instead of God is that of the spider that takes a home, and indeed the frailest of homes is the home of a spider, had they known![12]

In summary, if we wish for ethics to remain in a community such that it will strengthen the community and solidify its pillars; then these ethics must be built on a solid foundation. Every foundation is susceptible to collapse, except the foundation that is built on devotion to God because everything is perishable except God.

He sends down water from the sky whereat the valleys are flooded to [the extent of] their capacity, and the flood carries along a swelling scum. And from what they smelt in the fire for the purpose of [making] ornaments or wares, [there arises] a similar scum. That is how God compares truth and falsehood. As for the scum, it leaves as dross, and that which profits the people stays in the earth. That is how God draws comparisons. [13]

Impartiality in Moral Conduct

Dealing with people impartially, in your ethical conduct, is essential for the true establishment of ethics in society. It would be unethical to be truthful and honest to some people but dishonest in your dealings with others for no overriding necessity. Altruism loses some of its essence if it is only done for the benefit of some, excluding worthy others. The principles and values of ethics are standard and should be applied impartially. The Islamic faith relies on the premise that it is a necessity to have ethics implemented in socie-

---

[12] The Holy Quran. Chapter 29 [The Spider; Arabic: *Al-Ankaboot*]. Verse 41.
[13] The Holy Quran. Chapter 13 [The Thunder; Arabic: *Al-Raad*]. Verse 17.

ty without double standards. The Holy Quran emphasizes this justice, as it is one of the most important moral principles that safeguards nations and societies. It is noted that the cause for the destruction of some nations was their lack of justice and impartiality. The Holy Prophet (s) has been narrated to have said, "...*those before you were astray because if someone noble were to steal, they let him be; if someone weak were to steal, they would punish him*...*"*[14]

Islam refuses to implement ethical values forone group without impartially implementing them for another. Ethics must be applied impartially across all societies and all peoples, unlike the tradition of some groups that apply it when it is in the interest of their community but not when it conflicts with their selfish interests. Such groups applied standards and values that were not based on sound ethics when dealing with others. Take safety and security for example. God speaks of some groups who definitely provide safety and security to the people of their own faith, but do not bother to do the same for others.

> *Among the People of the Book is he who if you entrust him with a quintal will repay it to you, and among them is he who, if you entrust him with a dinar will not repay it to you unless you stand persistently over him. That is because they say, 'We have no obligation to the non-Jews.' But they attribute lies to God, and they know [it].*[15]

Islam rejects this type of differentiation in implementing the universal standard of ethics, and God considers these peo-

---

[14] Al-Tabarani, *Al-Mu'jam Al-Awsat*, 7:273; Al-Bukhari, *Saheeh Bukhari*, 8:16.
[15] The Holy Quran. Chapter 3 [Arabic: *Aal Imran*]. Verse 75.

ple to be blatantly lying about Him. "*Yes, whoever fulfills his commitments and is wary of God—God indeed loves the Godwary.*"[16]

Moreover, we find that Islam emphasizes the best of ethics even if it were to cause you personal loss or detriment. Losing one's personal interest for the sake of upholding justice and ethics could be seen in the example of being a just and proper witness.

> *O you who have faith! Be maintainers of justice and witnesses for the sake of God, even if it should be against yourselves or [your] parents and near relatives, and whether it be [someone] rich or poor, for God has a greater right over them. So do not follow [your] desires, lest you should be unfair, and if you distort [the testimony] or disregard [it], God is indeed well aware of what you do.*[17]

Justice is done when a person bears witness before God for God's sake and is not swayed by anyone. He comes forth with his testimony even to his own detriment, his family's, or relatives'. The fact that a person is poor or wealthy does not make a difference in regards to that testimony. The rights of a society are dependent on justice, equity, and upholding testimonies. Faith in God promotes this understanding in ethics without discrimination. Similarly, God speaks to the importance of fulfilling promises in contracts in the following verse: "*O you who have faith! Keep your agreements...*"[18] This verse is unrestricted in its command. It does not stipulate the obligation to contracts with Muslims or

---

[16] Ibid. Verse 76.

[17] The Holy Quran. Chapter 4 [The Women; Arabic: *Al-Nisaa*]. Verse 135.

[18] The Holy Quran. Chapter 5 [The Spread; Arabic: *Al-Maeda*]. Verse 1.

non-Muslims. This is the same when it comes to trusts and judgment:

> Indeed God commands you to deliver the trusts to their [rightful] owners, and to judge with fairness when you judge between people. Excellent indeed is what God advises you. Indeed God is all-hearing, all-seeing.[19]

Faith calls people to commit to these ethical principles and to act in accordance with them. This call is made for both self-dealing and dealing with others, without discrimination. When we look at our world today and see the culture of materialism that leads to double standards in its application of morals and ethics, it reinforces the idea that communities built on materialism will eventually fall because of their weak foundation which was not built on impartial ethics and faith.

Ethics as a Complete System

One of the fundamental aspects of ethics in our faith is that ethics, with all of its different elements, forms a complete system. Faith could not accept some of the virtues offered by ethics and leave other virtues. Rather, faith considers them all one system that is unable to be separated and partitioned. For as long as the driving force of all these ethical virtues is God, there would be no meaning in discriminating or separating between them. Moreover, faith suggests that all divine legislation and ethical virtues complement one another. This is due to the fact that divine legislation is based on the foundation of ethical virtues; based in mercy and goodness. He said,

---

[19] The Holy Quran. Chapter 4 [The Women; Arabic: *Al-Nisaa*]. Verse 58.

Indeed God enjoins justice and kindness, and generosity towards relatives, and He forbids indecency, wrongdoing, and aggression. He advises you, so that you may take admonition.[20]

From here we realize that people behaving with some virtues while neglecting others is similar to believing in parts of the Book while disbelieving other parts.

... Do you believe in part of the Book and deny another part? So what is the requital of those of you who do that except disgrace in the life of this world? And on the Day of Resurrection, they shall be consigned to the severest punishment. And God is not oblivious of what you do.[21]

Imam Al-Sadiq (a) beautifully showed this reality when he said, "*The characteristic of ethical virtues is that each virtue is tied to the other...*"[22]

With these formidable foundations, this system of ethics for the individual or the society will be a reason of strength for that individual or society. However, when ethics are not built on such foundations, divine order dictates that such a community will fall and collapse even with all its seeming strength and capability. In reality, that façade of strength may very well be the cause of its demise.

---

[20] The Holy Quran. Chapter 16 [The Bees; Arabic: *Al-Nahl*]. Verse 90.

[21] The Holy Quran. Chapter 2 [The Cow; Arabic: *Al-Baqara*]. Verse 85.

[22] Al-Majlisi, Bihar Al-Anwar, 66:375. From: Al-Tusi, Al-Amali, 301.

THE GOOD LIFE

In the name of God, the most Beneficent, the most Merciful

Whoever acts righteously, [whether] male or female, should he be faithful, We shall revive him with a good life and pay them their reward by the best of what they used to do.[1]

In this world we strive to have a good life, filled with comfort, calm, stability, happiness, and joy. This is very natural. It is an intrinsic inclination for humanity to want comfort, convenience, happiness, and stability. The distinction comes from the means through which we attain these things, and that differs from one person to the other. Most people do not achieve their aspirations, even though they work day and night to reach them. Instead of reaching 'the good life,' they take paths that take them astray internally and externally. They end up living a life without getting what they truly wanted. In some cases, they are able to get a hold of some tools that they think will grant them the happiness, stability and goodness they sought; but many times, those very tools are what cause them hardship and grief turning their whole life upside down. How many people think that money is

---

[1] The Holy Quran. Chapter 16 [The Bees; Arabic: *Al-Nahl*]. Verse 97.

their key to happiness and a good life? They work so hard throughout their life to make that money and watch it pile up, without realizing that they have become a slave to the very tool they thought would serve them. That money steals their joy, their comfort, their health, and their happiness. In reality, money does not allow them to enjoy anything at all.

Likewise, how many people think that they will reach 'the good life' by attaining power and prestige? Thus, they work to realize such a life even if it is at the expense of others and their happiness. They will not be able to attain a wholesome good life, and will in turn prevent it for others as well. This will lead to the worst life and the most miserable living. Such results are seen in this world. In the afterlife, which is the true life, such a person will in the same way bring upon himself his own punishment, pain and suffering. He will not realize and enjoy any type of life, here or later. Even if money and power were to give him anything in this life, he will definitely not realize anything in the next for the lack of his worth there.

So if money, prestige, power, and authority do not result in a good life, then what are the tools that the individual can use to actualize this goal of comfort and happiness in this life? Likewise, it is vital for a person to think of what will result in his happiness and comfort in the afterlife while he thinks of his happiness in this life. This is because, in reality, this life does not compare to the afterlife. *"The life of this world is nothing but diversion and play, but the abode of the Hereafter is indeed Life (itself), had they known!"*[2]

---

[2] The Holy Quran. Chapter 29 [The Spider; Arabic: *Al-Ankabout*]. Verse 64.

What are the tools that allow us to realize the good life both in this world and the next?

There is no doubt that a person is not able to reach the tools for happiness and stability without guidance and divine care. God created us. He knows us better than we know ourselves. He knows our potential, what is in our best interest, and what could destroy us. Thus, we would be gravely mistaken to embark on our journey towards happiness without consulting divine teachings and guidance. Perhaps one of the reasons for our failure to reach true happiness is that we take on paths that we think will bring us stability and happiness, but in reality go against our own interests. This is due to the fact that we may choose to have tunnel vision and limit our capacity.

God provides us with a group of fundamental elements upon which a good life may be founded. The most important of these elements are three: faith, submission to God, and contentment.

FAITH

Of the most significant elements to a person's stability and ensuring a wholesome life, is faith. Faith makes a person connected with everything. Faith connects one to his soul, his innate, his surroundings, and his entire world. Faith is the essence of stability in a person's life. Narrations from Ahlulbayt (a) point to this truth. Abu Hamza asked Imam Al-Baqir (a) about the verse in the Holy Quran that states,

"It is He who sent down composure into the hearts of the faithful..."[3]
The Imam (a) answered by saying, *"It is faith."*[4]

Thus, faith is tranquility and stability – two parts of having a good life. From this background it is essential to discuss a few more points:

How does faith bring a good life?

We believe that humanity was created for servitude, utmost devotion to God Almighty – the source of excellence in its entirety. Hence, all of mankind's tools and utilities, physical or spiritual, have the purpose of serving that primary goal. These tools and components have needs. On a physical level, people are in need of food, water, clothes, sexual release and other basic needs. People have spiritual needs as well, which go beyond just the physical senses, that are to be fulfilled on a spiritual level just the same.

God provided guidelines and limitations as to what will allow a person to fulfill both his physical and spiritual needs. This is all within a solid specific framework created for the human being to achieve and realize his purpose, which is through servitude and worship of God. Thus, if any defect or mistake take place on a physical or spiritual level, like eating forbidden foods, drinking alcohol, or having non-marital sex, they result in a defect in one's servitude. Whenever such a defect is to take place, a person is unable to fully engage with his innate nature. Rather, it is necessary for a person to walk this straight path in pursuit of that noble goal of reaching happiness and a good wholesome life. Such a path

---

[3] The Holy Quran. Chapter 48 [The Victory; Arabic: *Al-Fath*]. Verse 4.
[4] Al-Kulayni, Al-Kafi, 2:15

does not deviate from reason and common sense, which God created for us to embark on the journey to reach our happiness. Faith comes forth to push us in that direction whereby a life of happiness is realized.

There is only one to be worshipped and that is God. Humanity is in servitude of God and moves in the path of God's will. All of the components of the human being are engaged, both the physical and the spiritual, with what God has ordained in the system He created. By that, a person will live a life of comfort, happiness and stability.

The Holy Quran illustrates and clarifies this point via example, which is one of the frequently used methods used in the Quran to deliver an idea to the reader, in the following verse:

> *[It is] an Arabic Quran, without any deviousness, so that they may be Godwary. God draws an example: a man jointly owned by several contending masters, and a man belonging entirely to one man: are the two equal in comparison? All praise belongs to God! But most of them do not know.*[5]

Human beings were created for servitude and thus must fall in line with that purpose as servants to their Creator. As mentioned earlier, all the components of the human beings were made to engage with this fundamental reality. If we are to refuse our servitude to God, then we will inevitably become servants to someone or something else. In surveying any human being on Earth, it is impossible to find someone who is not actually in servitude to God or something else.

[5] The Holy Quran. Chapter 39 [The Crowds; Arabic: *Al-Zumar*]. Verses 28-29.

By 'something else,' it could be one's self, whimsical desires, power, money, or anything else. People who say that such a person is 'free' are kidding themselves. True freedom is not realized until a person is in complete service to God and only God. Otherwise, a person is still a slave to his desires, whims, and ignorance.

When a person believes and has faith in God, he is able to live in a state of stability and tranquility because he does not work for anything but the sake of God. And thus, all of the tools before him work seamlessly to achieve that noble goal. Without such faith, however, a person falls victim to the conflicting interests of the other 'gods' to which he is enslaved. Thus, he lives in a troubled state of instability, misery, and being torn away from what is innate and common sense. He loses the most important element of a good life – stability.

The type of faith that brings a good life

What is the faith that allows a person to realize a good life? Is superficially observed faith enough to realize this goal? Here we must address two fundamental issues and two significant points:

The required faith here is not theoretical in nature – if it is appropriate to use such a description. Rather, it is the faith referenced by the narrations of the Holy Prophet (s) and his Household (a) . The Holy Prophet (s) said, "*Faith is not through demonstrations and wishful thinking; rather, faith is what is concluded in the heart and confirmed in action.*"[6]

---

[6] Al-Saduq, *Ma'ani Al-Akhbar*, 187.

The Commander of the Faithful (a) said, *"The Holy Prophet (s) told me: 'Oh Ali write.' To that I said, 'What shall I write?' He said, 'Write in the Name of God the Beneficent the Merciful. Faith is what is revered in the hearts and confirmed in the deeds."*[7]

Thus, the faith that is required is the one that produces upright conduct or is confirmed by upright conduct. True faith is one that is owned by one whose actions are completely in sync with the conviction in his heart. The following verse professes this truth in its indication that righteous deeds and faith result in a good happy life. *"Whoever acts righteously, [whether] male or female, should he be faithful, We shall revive him with a good life and pay them their reward by the best of what they used to do."*[8]

Thus, theoretical faith or faith that is in one's heart alone is not enough to result in a happy life. Faith without action does not actualize true servitude to God. A state of engagement with one's inner soul will not be realized, and that person will remain a prisoner to his psychological troubles frustrating his life only further.

Faith has levels and degrees. The more a person increases in his degree of faith, the closer he becomes to reaching 'the good life.' The heart increases in its light and shines with what mandates the feelings of happiness. Imam Ali (a) said, *"Faith appears as a flash of light in the heart. When faith increases the flash of light also increases."*[9]

---

[7] Al-Majlisi, *Bihar Al-Anwar*, 50:208.

[8] The Holy Quran. Chapter 16 [The Bees; Arabic: *Al-Nahl*]. Verse 97.

[9] Al-Radi, *Nahj Al-Balagha*, 4:59.

Another narration of Imam Ali's (a) words goes into some more detail. *"Faith appears as a flashing white light in the heart. When one's faith increases in greatness, that whiteness in the heart also becomes greater. If one's faith is to be complete, his heart will whiten in its entirety."*[10]

When a person increases in his faith he also increases in his servitude to God, actualizing the true benefit from all of his faculties and energies in this journey. By that a person is able to realize a great deal of being truly engaged with one's inner self.

SUBMISSION TO GOD

In life, a person can experience two types of problems or hardships that he possibly may not understand causing him more difficulty and discomfort. Those are:

First: the necessity of restraint and commitment to the obligations and commands ordained by God. There is a big portion of this that a person may not completely understand, or may only know its superficial benefit. That in turn could make us feel constrained by these types of commands and responsibilities. If we choose not to commit to these responsibilities we feel like we have fallen out of God's favor by being disobedient. Beyond that guilt, there are many negative effects we experience by leaving obedience even before we die and move on to the next life. Nonetheless, if we do commit to following God's commands and fulfilling our obligations we may feel a sense of being restricted or constrained. We may tend to feel that our freedom is being

---

[10] Al-Hindi, *Kanz Al-'Amal*, 1:406, Tr. 1734.

infringed upon and the more we restrict ourselves with God's rules, the less free we become.

Second: we face many problems and tribulations in our lives that may seem like an annoyance and cause frustration for us. We find no clear explanation for these frustrations and we do not know their cause or reason. Generally, we tend to believe that happiness comes with the absence of any problems in our lives. Thus, when we see problems taking place and frustrations arise, we do not feel that we have a good stable life.

Every religious legislation and divine obligation given to us has a purpose of bringing forth a benefit or deflecting some type of harm to the individual. God is no need of our worship and servitude, he does not benefit nor is he harmed by people's quantity or quality of worship. The sole beneficiaries of servitude in relation to God are the servants themselves – us. Whether we worship God or not, the benefit or detriment only affects us, not God. The problems and tribulations we face are either caused by our own hands or given to us as a test of opportunity to show our nature to God. These tests are opportunities for us to increase our level or station both for this life and the next.

We are not capable of turning our feelings of fatigue, hardship, and difficulty in regards to these two issues to feelings of happiness, goodness, and contentment unless we channel them through submitting ourselves to God. We must prompt ourselves to see the reality that God only wants what is the best for us. He does not order us to do anything except that it is in our best interest. He does not test us except that such a test is good for us. By that we can realize true contentment. We can realize complete faith in God, because submitting to Him is the sign of faith and the greatest reflection of it. This sign is the distinction of a believer. Abi Abdillah (a) was asked how does one know that someone is a believer. To that the Imam (a) responded, *"By submission to God, and contentment in what he experiences in both times of joy and times of indignation."*[11]

The Holy Quran denies the designation of faith to those people who do not submit to the rule of God and His Prophet.

> *But no, by your Lord! They will not believe until they make you a judge in their disputes, then do not find within their hearts any dissent to your verdict and submit in full submission.*[12]

All in all, submission to God in all matters will result in experiencing 'the good life.' This servitude to God results in true faith and the highest levels of it. When a person is in a state of objection to God's will, he is not able to change his reality, rather he will stay living in pain and strain. On the other hand, with submission to His will and contentment, it naturally mandates the feelings of tranquility and comfort. Not to forget, such servitude to God results in being rewarded by God both in this life and the next. Divine Wisdom means that God's commands are based on real benefits to be gained and real harms to be avoided, both in this world and the Hereafter. All of these elements play into the natural result of reaching the goal of happiness and living a good life.

---

[11] Al-Kulayni, *Al-Kafi*, 2:63.
[12] The Holy Quran. Chapter 4 [The Women; Arabic: *Al-Nisaa*]. Verse 65.

In many supplications taught to us by Ahlulbayt (a), we ask God to grant us contentment in everything that God gives us. For example, in 'Ziyarat Ameen God' – a ziyara that is well known and attributed to our Holy Imams (a) – we find this phrase: *"O' God, make me self-assured with your magnitude, and content with your judgment..."*

The narrations of Ahlulbayt (a) clearly indicate that submitting to God and delegating the fate of your affairs to Him mandates psychological comfort for the individual, which is one of the most important elements to living a happy life.

Imam Al-Baqir (a) told Jabbir Al-Ju'fi, *"...Allow yourself psychological comfort with delegation [of your affairs to God]..."*[13] In another narration, Imam Al-Sadiq (a) was noted to have said, *"The person who delegates his affair to God, is in eternal comfort and a state of durable lasting living..."*[14]

CONTENTMENT

Contentment is of the greatest causes of comfort in this life and the afterlife. It has been reported that in some of the exegeses of the Holy Prophet (s) and his Ahlulbayt (a) that they explained the following: The good life comes with contentment. The author of Mujamma' Al-Bayan explained the verse *"We shall revive him with a good life..."*[15]

> One of the meanings are: the good life, lawful sustenance, as narrated from Ibn Abbas and Saeed bin Jubayr and 'Ataa. The second meaning: it is contentment and accepting

---

[13] Al-Harrani, *Tohaf Al-'Oqool*, 285.

[14] *Misbah Al-Sharee'a*, 175 (the book is attributed to Imam Al-Sadiq (a)).

[15] The Holy Quran. Chapter 16 [The Bees; Arabic: *Al-Nahl*]. Verse 97.

what God has ordained, as narrated from Al-Hassan (a) and Wahab, which was also narrated from the Holy Prophet (sa)...[16]

This has also been narrated from the Commander of the Faithful (a) when he was asked about the same verse mentioned above. To that he said, *"It is contentment."*[17]

We find this emphasis on contentment because generally many people are discontent with what they have. No matter how much they attain, they still want more. Imam Al-Sadiq (a) said, *"...If the son of Adam had two valleys filled with gold and silver, he would still wish for a third one. O' son of Adam, your stomach is a sea and a valley - nothing will fill it up but the soil."*[18]

Some people always feel this sense of lacking or deficiency, for no matter how much they get they continue to want more. This sense of deficiency adds to their troubles and makes them worry over their share in this life. They will work day and night to gather their wealth or climb the ladder of power, becoming so fixated and causing themselves spiritual ailments. Greed, envy, bullying, and infringing on other people's rights are all natural effects of discontentment. Each one of these spiritual ailments causes pain. Thus, they convince themselves that they will not feel any better unless they get richer. They do not realize that true richness is an internal feeling of stability that we call contentment. A person who is content is rich, and because of that richness he feels happiness. Without contentment that same person is poor, no matter how much money he has.

---

[16] Al-Tabrasi, *Mujamma' Al-Bayan*, 6:198.

[17] Al-Radi, *Nahj Al-Balagha*, 4:51.

[18] Al-Saduq, *Man La Yahduruh Al-Faqih*, 4:418, Tr. 5912.

Narrations of Ahlulbayt (a) confirm this idea that the true richness that causes happiness is contentment, not money or wealth. Imam Ali (a) said, *"I requested richness and only found it through contentment. Through contentment you will find richness..."*[19]

God advised Prophet David (a) as follows: *"O' David, I have placed five things in five, and people look for them in five other things but do not find what they are looking for... I have placed richness in contentment. People look for richness in money, but they will not find it..."*[20]

In summary, richness is without a doubt one of the causes for comfort, happiness, and a good life. But richness, in accordance to our noble traditions, is something that comes from within. It is an internal state that a person has, whenever he is in that state he feels rich. Without that internal stability, he feels impoverished even if he owns the entire world. There is no doubt that poverty is a cause for human suffering. A person cannot feel the goodness of life in a state of poverty. But poverty here is not measured by wealth, it is measured by contentment. It is true that a human being has natural physical needs and if they are not fulfilled then the person may not function with the best judgment. But when the bare minimum of one's needs are met, contentment is the key to richness, and discontentment naturally mandates destitution. Contentment, submission to God, and faith are the three fundamental elements to securing a good and happy life.

---

[19] Al-Majlisi, *Bihar Al-Anwar*, 66:399, Tr. 91.
[20] Al-Hilli, *'Uddat Al-Da'ee*, 166.

STRUGGLE WITHIN

In the name of God, the most Beneficent, the most Merciful

*As for those who strive in Us, We shall surely guide them
in Our ways, and God is indeed with the virtuous.*[1]

Before we begin our discussion about the topic of "struggle
with the self" and the reality of this great struggle that the
Prophet (s) called "the Greater Jihad," we must point to a
few key concepts as an introduction:

A Breakdown

First, each individual, throughout their existence, passes
through a number of stages. Perhaps the shortest of these
stages is life in this world. If we were to look at the ratio of
life in the womb to life in this world, and compare it to the
ratio of the life in this world to life in the hereafter, we find
that the ratios are very divergent. No matter how long a
person may live on this world, the value of life on this world
is nothing compared to life in the hereafter – after all, the
life of the hereafter is boundless and eternal. And because

---

[1] The Holy Quran. Chapter 29 [The Spider; Arabic: *Al-Ankaboot*]. Verse 69.

this comparison is so dramatic, God described this world as one of play and distraction. God says, *"The life of this world is nothing but diversion and play, but the abode of the Hereafter is indeed Life (itself), had they known!"*[2]

God also tells us how insignificant the pleasures of this world are compared to those of the hereafter – *"Are you pleased with the life of this world instead of the Hereafter? But the wares of the life of this world compared with the Hereafter are but insignificant."*[3] No matter how long and hard people may work to secure their life in this world, in the end everyone will pass to the other world where their happiness is contingent on their path and life in this world.

Second, true happiness is attained only in the eternal hereafter, and only in attaining closeness to God and His pleasure. That is the highest level of achievement and success, as the Holy Quran clearly states:

> God has promised the faithful, men and women, gardens with streams running in them, to remain in them [forever], and good dwellings in the Gardens of Eden. Yet God's pleasure is greater [than all these]; that is the great success.[4]

This stature cannot be attained by any individual except through his choices in this life and the constant struggle to attain closeness to God (SWT). Indeed, nothing in the hereafter can be attained except through struggle in this world. God reminds us of this truth in his Holy Book:

---

[2] Ibid. Verse 64.
[3] The Holy Quran. Chapter 9 [The Repentance; Arabic: *Al-Tawba*]. Verse 38.
[4] Ibid. Verse 72.

Has he not been informed of what is in the scriptures of Moses, and of Abraham, who fulfilled [his summons]: that no bearer shall bear another's burden, that nothing belongs to man except what he strives for, and that he will soon be shown his endeavor, then he will be rewarded for it with the fullest reward.[5]

One cannot reach closeness to God or attain His pleasure except through the great struggle of this world. Rather, God's guidance and his direct blessings and direction cannot be achieved except through this struggle. *"As for those who strive in Us, We shall surely guide them in Our ways, and God is indeed with the virtuous."*[6]

Third, every individual must go through this struggle with the great enemy; the one who promised to ambush us at every corner and on every path that leads towards God. We read in the Quran the story of our enemy Satan, as he speaks to God:

I will surely lie in wait for them on Your straight path. Then I will come at them from their front and from their rear, and from their right and their left, and You will not find most of them to be grateful.[7]

This enemy will not stop. He will take any measure to deprive mankind of the great happiness that God wanted for them. Alongside him is a greater enemy; the self and its desires. God describes the state of mankind thus: *"Yet I do not absolve my [own carnal] soul, for the [carnal] soul indeed prompts*

---

[5] The Holy Quran. Chapter 53 [The Star; Arabic: *Al-Najm*]. Verses 36-41.
[6] The Holy Quran. Chapter 29 [The Spider; Arabic: *Al-Ankaboot*]. Verse 69.
[7] The Holy Quran. Chapter 7 [The Heights; Arabic: *Al-Araf*]. Verses 16 and 17.

[men] to evil, except inasmuch as my Lord has mercy. Indeed my Lord is all-forgiving, all-merciful.[8] Indeed, the narrations of the Holy Household of the Prophet have told us about the great dangers of the self. It is narrated that the Prophet (s) even said *"Your worst enemy is your self that is within you."*[9]

The process of struggle is continuous and will not stop for a single moment. From the time that a person reaches the point of maturity and religious obligation to the point that he or she passes to the next world, no one can desert this battlefield. There is no truce that can be reached with this enemy. This battle differs from all the rest that are waged between men. In other wars, all parties will find time to rest, a truce might be reached, and even a peace treaty may be signed. In this battle, all this is impossible. Any pause in the battle will only mean defeat. Any truce is an even greater defeat. For this reason, the Prophet (s) called this the greater struggle.

Indeed, this struggle is greater in both hardships and in rewards. In a normal war, the greatest that can befall anyone is death – and death is merely a transition from one world to another. But in the case of the great struggle for self-purification, a defeat could mean a life in God's wrath. Furthermore, there is no choice of retreat in the greater struggle, as any retreat will only mean defeat.

Fourth, although this is a dangerous and vigorous battle, we should all keep in perspective the following two points:

---

[8] The Holy Quran. Chapter 12 [Joseph; Arabic: *Yousef*]. Verse 53.
[9] Al-Majlisi, *Bihar Al-Anwar*, 67:36.

Firstly, we should at all times remind ourselves of the weakness of these two enemies. Satan is an especially weak enemy, as he can never gain control over anyone unless that person willingly gives up control to him. God refers to the weakness of Satan on many occasions in His Holy Book, such as in the verse *"Those who have faith fight in the way of God, and those who are faithless fight in the way of fake gods. So fight the friends of Satan; indeed the stratagems of Satan are always flimsy."*[10] God also tells us that Satan has no power over us: *"Indeed, as for My servants you do not have any authority over them, except the perverse who follow you,"*[11] and *"'As for My servants, you shall have no authority over them.' And your Lord suffices as trustee."*[12] Satan even admits this himself, as is narrated in the Holy Quran:

> *When the matter is all over, Satan will say, 'Indeed God made you a promise that was true and I [too] made you a promise, but I failed you. I had no authority over you, except that I called you and you responded to me. So do not blame me, but blame yourselves. I cannot respond to your distress calls, neither can you respond to my distress calls. Indeed I disavow your taking me for [God's] partner aforetime. There is indeed a painful punishment for the wrongdoers.*[13]

As for the second enemy – the sinful self – there is an exception to its deviance. The sinful self *"indeed prompts [men] to evil, except inasmuch as my Lord has mercy. Indeed my Lord is all-forgiving, all-merciful."*[14] To enter into this exception of mercy,

---

[10] The Holy Quran, Chapter 4 [The Women; Arabic: *Al-Nisaa*], Verse 76.

[11] The Holy Quran, Chapter 15 [The Stoneland; Arabic: *Al-Hijr*], Verse 42.

[12] The Holy Quran, Chapter 17 [The Ascendance; Arabic: *Al-Israa*], Verse 65.

[13] The Holy Quran, Chapter 14 [Abraham; Arabic: *Ibrahim*], Verse 22.

[14] The Holy Quran, Chapter 12 [Joseph; Arabic: *Yousef*], Verse 53.

the self must take the right stand in this great battle between truth and falsehood.

Secondly, we must realize that there is a means to reach a decisive victory in this battle, and that is through seeking aid and having reliance on God (SWT) during the battle. If a person was to connect to this infinite source of power that is incomparable to any other, victory will surely be on his side. The Holy Quran is filled with promises of victory for whoever wants closeness to God and does indeed take the side that God desired for him in this battle.

God says: *"As for those who strive in Us, We shall surely guide them in Our ways, and God is indeed with the virtuous."*[15] He also says:

> *Whoever is wary of God, He shall make for him a way out [of the adversities of the world and the Hereafter] and provide for him from whence he does not count upon. And whoever puts his trust in God, He will suffice him. Indeed God carries through His commands. Certainly, God has ordained a measure [and extent] for everything.*[16]

Keeping these points in mind will allow us to better understand the reality of the struggle that we all face.

THE PARTIES

Scholars of ethics have characterized the struggle as a prolonged war between the forces of good and the forces of evil. The struggle has also been characterized as a war between the soldiers of God and the soldiers of Satan. If an

---

[15] The Holy Quran, Chapter 29 [The Spider; Arabic: *Al-Ankaboot*], Verse 69.
[16] The Holy Quran, Chapter 65 [Divorce; Arabic: *Al-Talaq*], Verses 2 and 3.

individual's faculties choose the side of good led by the sound intellect, they are the soldiers of God. But if the faculties stand on the side of evil led by the force of ignorance, they become the soldiers of Satan. When the faculties stand on the side of good and virtue, they are also called the soldiers of the intellect, as the intellect is the leader of those forces. Otherwise, they become the soldiers of ignorance, as ignorance is the leader on that side of the battle.

Therefore, we must seek to understand the reality of the intellect and ignorance as the leading forces in this battle. For this reason, we see such an emphasis in narrations on the importance of understanding these forces – Imam Sadiq (a) said *"know the intellect and its soldiers, and ignorance and its soldiers, and you will be guided."*[17]

The Intellect

Scholars of ethics have differing perspectives on the reality of the intellect. However, a general understanding of the intellect can be derived from the following two roles:

The first role of the intellect is that of awareness and discernment. And it is this intellect that separates mankind from other animals. The intellect is what allows us to learn the empirical sciences and to engage in logical argumentation. It also allows us to discern and differentiate between good and evil.

So the intellect is what allows us to discern and differentiate between good and evil and understand cause and effect, and balance considerations and consequences. And for that reason, we say that a reasonable person – someone who uses

---

[17] Al-Kulayni, *Al-Kafi*, 1:21 (The Book of Intellect and Ignorance).

reason and intellect – is the person who foresees the ends and consequences of any matter. And this is what distinguishes us from other animals. A reasonable individual does not look at the immediate satisfaction of an action only, but will see and think about other consequences beyond that. How many good tasting drinks do we see on the market that can cause us illness? And how many bad tasting drinks do we see that can be the cure for our illnesses? Each individual uses his reasoning ability to judge which of these products to drink and when.

And because of this great capacity to reason that is given to us through our intellect, it is said the intellect is the key to both paradise and hellfire. And this idea has reached us in a number of narrations, such as the narration of Imam Baqir (a) describing the creation of the intellect:

> *When God created the intellect He gave it the ability to speak. He then asked it to come forth and it did. He asked it to go back and it did. He then told it 'by My Honor and Glory, I have not created anything more beloved to me than you, and I have not completed you except in those that I love. Indeed, I command you and prohibit you, and I will punish you and reward you.*[18]

When Imam Sadiq (a) was asked about the intellect, he replied *"it is [the tool] which is used to worship the Merciful [Lord] and earn his paradise."*[19]

This ability to distinguish between good and evil, and between virtue and vice, bears a great mark on humanity. So

---

[18] Ibid. 1:10.
[19] Ibid. 1:11.

much so, that it is a foundation for legislation, such that a person who does not have the ability to reason – a person who is "insane" or "mentally incompetent" – is not held to the standards that are imposed by law. In the same way, God's commands also revolve around the intellect and sanity of the individual. So it is that ability to reason that allows us to gain closeness to God and to acquire a good character.

One may wonder "if the intellect is the tool that brings us closer to God, then why do we see so many rational individuals, such as scientists and engineers, who have not gained an understanding and a closeness to God?" The answer will be understood through our discussions on the second role of the intellect and the reality of ignorance.

The second role of the intellect is that of driving actions in accordance with reason. The intellect does not simply supply us with knowledge of different options that we can choose. But to be a rational individual, you must not only understand these choices, but also choose good over evil. So reason is a combination of both knowledge and action, as will be clear in our discussion of ignorance.

Ignorance

Some may think that ignorance is simply a lack of knowledge, so that a person who does not know something is called ignorant. In reality, "ignorance,"[20] as was discussed in the narrations, is a positive concept – it asserts the existence of something – rather than a negative concept that only asserts the lack of knowledge. Ignorance is the opposite of intellect. Ignorance, in fact, is a state of knowledge with-

---

[20] Arabic: *al-jahl.*

out action. It is a state of the self that drives a person to choose what is evil and harmful over what is good and beneficial. It is a state of the self that drives a person to succumb to carnal desires.

This meaning is clearly found in the narrations of the Holy Household of the Prophet (s). Imam Sadiq (a) was asked "what is intellect?" He replied "*it is a tool used for the worship of God and earning a place in Paradise.*" The Imam was asked about the oppressors and whether they had an intellect. He replied "*vice and Satanic wit. They are similar to the intellect, but they are not a form of intellect.*"[21]

So what people casually call "intellect" is not the same intellect that is described in the narrations of the Prophet (s) and his Holy Household (a). Not anyone who has a form of wit or cunning possesses this intellect. On the contrary, if a person has some knowledge but does not act in accordance with it, then that person has reached the peak of ignorance. That ignorance will lead to hellfire no matter how many religious slogans the person has memorized. Imam Ali (a) describes such a person as the most ignorant; he says:

> *While the other kind of man [as opposed to the believer] is he who calls himself learned but he is not so. He has gleaned ignorance from the ignorant and misguidance from the misguided. He has set for the people a trap made of the ropes of deceit and falsehood. He takes the Qur'an according to his own views and bends the truth to suit his passions. He makes people feel safe from great sins and takes lightly the most serious crimes. He says that he holds back in the face*

---

[21] Al-Barqi, *Al-Mahasin*, 1:195, Tr. 15.

of doubtful matters while he is plunged in them, and he says that he keeps aloof from innovations while he is actually immersed in them. His shape is that of a man, but his heart is that of a beast. He does not know the door of guidance to follow nor the door of misguidance to keep aloof therefrom. These are the dead [minds with] living bodies.

So we realize that the use of the word "intellect" in the narrations of the Holy Household is different from its use in the studies of philosophy and logic, where the term is meant to describe the ability to perceive. Hence, our scholars of ethics characterize the intellect as both an ability to distinguish between good and evil, and a force that drives towards good and away from evil.

The Virtues

With that framework in mind, we are able to see an inseparable connection between the intellect and a number of virtues. This is reinforced in a number of narrations, such as in the words of Imam Ali (a):

Gabriel (a) descended on Adam (a) and said 'Oh Adam, I have been commanded to give you the choice between one of three options, so choose one and leave the others.' So Adam replied 'Oh Gabriel, what are the three choices?' Gabriel answered 'intellect, modesty, and faith'. Adam said 'I choose the intellect.' So Gabriel turned to modesty and faith and told them 'go and leave him.' They replied 'Oh Gabriel, we have been commanded to be with the intellect wherever it goes.' He said 'it is up to you' and ascended to the Heavens.[22]

---

[22] Al-Kulayni, *Al-Kafi*, 1:10 (The Book of Intellect and Ignorance).

Because the intellect is a force that recognizes good and drives the individual towards it, it inevitably will lead the individual towards modesty. A rational individual will no doubt gravitate towards an ethic of modesty that would deter him from falling into vice. So alongside the intellect that drives towards what is good, modesty will be there to deter the individual from sin.

Another virtue that will accompany the intellect is that of faith. Faith and piety will drive the individual closer to what is good and will also deter him from falling into sin. As one scholar of ethics characterizes it, faith is "'the straight path' that will take anyone traveling on it closer to virtue and away from vice. [Faith] is knowledge of the totality of factors that brings a person closer to the Lord and acting on His commands, as well as knowledge of the totality of factors that lead the individual away from God and not falling into what has been prohibited."[23]

Therefore, any individual who maintains a true intellect will earn many more virtues that will light up his path to happiness and contentment and aid him in his struggle with the self. In this struggle with ignorance and its soldiers, modesty and faith will always be on the other side. With every degree of ignorance comes a degradation in degrees of modesty and faith.

As for communities that are entrenched in evil and corruption, you will not see them have either of these virtues. The dissolution of ethics and the rampant social corruption will drive an individual to a point where all modesty is lost, even

---

[23] Al-Mazandarani, *Sharh Usool Al-Kafi*, 1:73.

if that person has reached a high level of knowledge. So the intellect is something very different from mere knowledge, as is clear from the words of the Holy Household. Societies that have high scientific and technological achievements will remain ignorant societies from our perspective because they lack the forces that drive towards good and that deter from evil and corruption. These societies that lack modesty and faith do not differ in their ignorance from the ignorance of Arabia before Islam, where faith, modesty, and the drive towards virtue were nonexistent.

THE BATTLEGROUND

After understanding the reality of the two opposing forces in this battle for self purification, let us look at the remaining faculties of the human self. On the one hand, these faculties serve as the battlefield as the forces of intellect and the forces of ignorance are fighting for control of these faculties. On the other hand, these faculties can serve as troops in this battle for whichever side has gained control over them. These faculties can either lead to the greatest of successes if they are controlled by the forces of the intellect, or they could lead to the ultimate defeat if they are controlled by the forces of ignorance. As for the faculties, they are as follows:

Desire

Desire is a faculty of great importance within the human self. There are two essential acts that are undertaken by this faculty.

Appetite. The first act undertaken by the faculty of desire is to satisfy the appetite for food and drink. The act of eating is essential to human life, both physiologically and socially. If we did not consume any food, we would not be able to sustain our bodies and continue to live in this world. And because the body is a tool through which the soul acts, the soul's worldly actions depend on the living body. Therefore, a healthy diet is essential not only to sustain the living body, but also for the continued activity of the soul in this world. Furthermore, our natural desire to satisfy our appetite is a means to reflect on and appreciate the blessings of God bestowed upon us through food and drink.

Yet this faculty does not have the ability to reason. Its only goal is to consume. It does not distinguish between *halal* and *haram*, or between little and plenty, or the effects that each of these would have on the body and the self. It only seeks to be satisfied and nourish the body through consumption. Therefore, there must be another faculty that controls this one and organizes its affairs; or else it would cause many problems for the individual on both a physical and a metaphysical level. And here lies the role of the intellect in regulating and supporting this faculty, so that it only acts in a way that is beneficial to the body and the soul. We see many narrations that emphasize the importance of food and its effect on the human body and soul. The body is connected to the human soul and the soul, at the level of the body, develops along with it. Therefore, if the body is nurtured with pure *halal* food, the soul will also be purified. But if the body grows on impure and *haram* food, that will lead to the impurity and corruption of the soul.

The narrations that pertain to food focus on a number of things:

1. The effects on the body, which consequently has an effect on the soul; especially since the body is the primary tool for the soul's physical actions: That is why we see an emphasis on refraining from overeating because of the negative effects it has on the body, and, consequently, on the soul. The Commander of the Faithful Imam Ali (a) in his will to his son Imam Hasan (a) said *"Oh son, would you like me to teach you four characteristics that will allow you to live without need for medicine?"* Imam Hasan (a) replied *"Yes, Oh Commander of the Faithful."* Imam Ali said *"Do not sit at a table to eat except when you are hungry. Always leave the table while you still crave the food. Chew well. If you want to go to sleep, use the restroom first. If you follow this advice, you will not need medicine."*[24] Imam Ali (a) also said *"beware of addiction to satisfying the appetite fully, for it riles ailments and brings about illnesses."*[25]

2. The effects on the soul due to diet: There is a number of narrations that point to the effects that food can have on the self and the role that it can play in stifling spiritual growth. It is narrated that the Prophet (s) said *"do not kill your hearts with overeating and overdrinking, for the heart dies much like a plant if overwatered."*[26] It is also narrated that the Prophet (s) said *"do not satisfy your appetite fully such that the light of*

---

[24] Al-Saduq, *Al-Khisal*, 229.

[25] Al-Nuri, *Mustadrak Al-Wasa'el*, 16:221.

[26] Al-Tabrasi, *Makarim Al-Akhlaq*, 15.

knowledge in your hearts is extinguished. Whoever prays with a light stomach is joined by the heavenly maidens."[27]

3. Emphasis on the purity and permissibility of the food, as that has a great effect on the movement of the soul towards God: It is narrated that the Prophet (s) said *"whoever eats halal food, an angel hovers over his head and prays for him until he finishes his meal."*[28] It is also narrated that the Prophet (s) said *"whoever eats halal food for forty days, God will enlighten his heart."*[29] He (s) also said *"worship combined with eating haram food is like building a structure over sand."*[30]

So we see that food is integral to self-purification. The desire for food is a blessing given by God, without which we cannot sustain a suitable body for the soul to use.

Sexual Desire. The second act undertaken by the faculty of desire is to satisfy sexual impulses. This desire is integral for the continuity of the human race and the advancement of societies. It is also a means for humans to appreciate the physical beauty of God's creation. However, it must always be under control, as it does not distinguish between *halal* and *haram*. It seeks gratification and satisfaction by any means possible. Therefore, the intellect must be in control of this desire so that it is only used within the bounds of religious guidelines that guide and reinforce the intellect. There is a great deal of narrations that address this desire from a number of aspects – including the importance of

---

[27] Al-Majlisi, *Bihar Al-Anwar*, 63:331.

[28] Ibid. 66:314.

[29] Ibid. 100:16.

[30] Ibid. 81:258.

allowing permissible means of satisfaction of this impulse, the religious guidelines regulating it, the manners and traditions associated with it, and warning of satisfying this desire through impermissible means. The teachings of our religion stress the importance of safeguarding this faculty through marriage and the need to satisfy the desire through legitimate means. This not only aids the reproductive purpose of sexual desire, but also has its own rewards in the hereafter. Religious teachings regard early marriage as a tradition that must be preserved, as has been related in the narration of Imam Sadiq (a):

> *The wife of Othman ibn Mazoun came to the Prophet (s) and said 'oh Messenger of God, Othman spends his days fasting and his nights worshipping.' The Messenger of God left angered carrying his shoes and came to Othman and found him praying. When Othman saw the Prophet (s) he cut short his prayers and turned to the Prophet (s). The Prophet (s) told him 'Oh Othman, God did not send me as a messenger to preach monasticism. Rather He sent me with an upright, easy, and tolerant religion. I fast and pray, but I am also intimate with my family. So whoever loves my innate nature let him follow my tradition, and marital relations are of my tradition.*[31]

We should also point out the solemn warnings against allowing this desire to have full reign and freedom. It is enough to point to fornication as one method of fulfilling this desire through impermissible means, and the effects that such actions can have on the individual. Our texts contain many references to this, including God's words *"Do not*

---

[31] Al-Kulayni, *Al-Kafi*, 5:494.

approach fornication. It is indeed an indecency and an evil way."[32] Imam Sadiq (a) also says:

> *The fornicator possesses six traits, three of them are in this world and three are in the hereafter. In this world, fornication removes the light of the face, begets poverty, and hastens death. As for the hereafter, it will incur the wrath of God, a terrible judgment, and an eternity in hellfire.*[33]

Indeed, without life-changing regret and repentance, fornication is spiritually lethal. Imam Kadhim (a) also said "*beware of fornication, for it eliminates blessings and nullifies faith.*"[34] And there are many other narrations in regards to fornication and other impermissible methods of fulfilling this desire. Of course, if one repents sincerely, God's mercy extends to those willing to receive it.

Controlling the Desires. In summary, the faculty of desire is one of the most important faculties in the human self and it must be under the control of the intellect. Whenever a person is able to control it, it will become a force that drives him toward excellence and elevation. It will lead to the victory of the forces of God over the forces of Satan within the human soul. However, if a person is not able to control this desire and allows it to reign freely, that will lead him to succumb to a level that is lower than that of savage beasts with no intellect; this amazing power of the intellect with which we humans have been endowed and were asked to place all faculties under its control.

---

[32] The Holy Quran, Chapter 17 [The Ascension; Arabic: *Al-Israa*], Verse 32.
[33] Al-Kulayni, *Al-Kafi*, 5:541.
[34] Ibid. 5:542.

One might ask "If these desires are so hard to control – as we see the much of the world living in a state of sin – why did God not create us without it so that we can be completely obedient to Him?"

God's wisdom has dictated the creation of three categories of being: one with an intellect and no desire and those are the angels; one with desires and no intellect, and those are the animals; and one with both desires and an intellect and that is us humans.

Whenever a person is able to allow his intellect to control his desires, he is elevated to a status that is higher than the angels – that is the status of the prophets and the righteous. However, if a person allows his desires to take control, he will slip and descend into a status that is lower than that of the animals. God says in his Holy Book, *"Do you suppose that most of them listen or exercise their reason? They are just like cattle; indeed, they are further astray from the way."*[35] So the purpose of humankind is to become better than the angels and to reach higher levels, and that can be reached through subjection of the desires to the intellect. When a person struggles to purify himself and faces his desires and temptations, this struggle will take him higher through the levels of closeness to God. It is a means to reach God. Therefore, the existence of these desires is itself a blessing from this perspective, alongside the physical ends that are reached through the desire.

---

[35] The Holy Quran, Chapter 25 [Arabic: *Al-Furqan*], Verse 44.

Anger

Anger is one of the important faculties within the human self, and it has a great deal of influence on the individual.

The Significance of Anger. The issue of anger is one that is given great attention within the faith. Anger is a force which, if controlled by the intellect, can push an individual further towards excellence. However, if the force of anger is not controlled, it can lead to great harm for the individual and everything around him. One look at the history of mankind will clearly show this, as we see petty disputes leading to the deaths of millions of individuals. We find that most of these atrocities were driven by anger. Human life is so dear to God, as He says:

> *That is why We decreed for the Children of Israel that whoever kills a soul, without [its being guilty of] manslaughter or corruption on the earth, is as though he had killed all mankind, and whoever saves a life is as though he had saved all mankind. Our apostles certainly brought them manifest signs, yet even after that, many of them commit excesses on the earth.[36]*

Yet this force of anger has led to the death of so many of mankind. The words of God and the narrations of the Prophet (s) and His Holy Household (a) are meant to direct our attention to the great importance of this force and the grave danger that it can pose.

It is narrated that Imam Sadiq (a) said:

---

[36] The Holy Quran, Chapter 5 [The Banquet, Arabic: *Al-Ma'ida*], Verse 32.

A nomad came to the Prophet (s) and said 'I live in the de-
sert and I would like to learn from you the best of wisdom.'
The Prophet replied 'I command you to never become angry.'
The nomad asked the same question three times [and re-
ceived the same answer]. Finally the nomad said 'I will nev-
er ask about anything else. The Prophet (s) has given me
the best of commands.' My father [Imam Baqir (a)] would
also say 'What is worse than anger? A man would get mad
and reach a point where he kills a soul with disregard to its
sanctity or defame a chaste woman.'[37]

This is a clear indication that anger is a key to vice. Rather, as is narrated from Imam Sadiq (a), anger is *"the key to all evil."*[38]

The narrations also indicate that rage is a satanic impulse. The state of loss of temper that takes a person out of his sound mind is a satanic state. However, the force of anger is not satanic in its entirety. Rather, it is rage that is a soldier of Satan. It is narrated that the Commander of the Faithful (a) wrote to Harith Al-Hamadani *"beware of rage, as it is a great soldier of Satan."*[39] Imam Baqir (a) also confirmed that rage is a satanic vice, as it is narrated that he said *"Rage is an ember that Satan places in the sons of Adam, so that if a person becomes enraged his eyes become red and his veins bulge, and Satan enters his body."*[40]

Controlling Anger. The narrations emphasize the importance of controlling anger as a means of taking it from a

---

[37] Al-Kulayni, *Al-Kafi*, 2:303.
[38] Ibid.
[39] Al-Radi, *Nahj Al-Balagha*, 3:131, Letter 69.
[40] Al-Kulayni, *Al-Kafi*, Volume 2:304.

malicious force to one of good and one that drives a person towards happiness. The Prophet (s) and his Holy Progeny (a) have taught us the importance of controlling our anger, and the importance of keeping this force and passion under control. Their teachings can be split into three categories:

First, the importance and the positive effects of controlling anger. It is narrated that Imam Sadiq once said:

> *The Prophet (s) once passed by a group of people lifting a boulder. He asked them what they were doing. They said that we use this to know who is the strongest and most powerful among us. So the Prophet (s) said 'would you like me to tell you who is the strongest and most powerful amongst you?' They replied 'Yes, oh Prophet of God.' The Prophet (s) said 'the strongest and most powerful is the one who, when content, his contentment would not cause him to fall into sin or vice. If he were to become angry, his anger would not stop him from saying the truth. If he has power, he will not take anything that is not rightfully his.* [41]

It is also narrated that the Prophet (s) once said, "*the most powerful is not the one who can beat others in wrestling. Rather the most powerful is the one who can maintain control of himself during anger.*"[42]

Second, the negative effects of not standing up to anger and being controlled by it. It is narrated that Imam Ali (a) said, "*bad temper is a strike of insanity. Whoever goes through it must feel regret. If he does not regret, then insanity has taken hold of him.*"[43] It

---

[41] Al-Saduq, *Ma'ani Al-Akhbar*, 366.

[42] Al-Harrani, *Tohaf Al-'Oqool*, 47.

[43] Al-Radi, *Nahj Albalagha*, 4:57, Saying 255.

is also narrated that he said, *"whoever becomes controlled by his anger and his desires has stooped to the ranks of the beasts."*[44]

Third, curing the problem of anger. Anger takes a person away from his normal demeanor and allows him to lose control of himself. Therefore, the person must be able to take control again through his actions. It is narrated that the Prophet (s) once told Imam Ali, *"Oh Ali, do not be angry. If you were to become angry, sit down and think about the power of your Lord over his subjects and His benevolence towards them. If someone tells you 'beware of God,' discard your anger and go back to your benevolence."*[45]

The cure to anger is the remembrance of God, His power, and His patience. The cure to anger is a theoretical one. Al-lama Majlisi says, "Know that the cure to anger is either theoretical or practical. The theoretical cure comes through remembrance of the verses and narrations that disparage anger and praise patience, forgiveness, and benevolence. Think of your expectation for God's mercy and his patience towards him."[46]

The practical cure consists of taking actions that distract the person from his anger and allow him to take back control of himself. This cure has been conveyed to us in the narrations of the Holy Household of the Prophet (s). The narration of Imam Baqir (a) says, *"A man may become angry and never regain his temper until he sees hellfire. If a man were to become angry, let him sit down immediately, as that will drive away the evil of Satan...."*[47]

---

[44] Al-Nuri, *Mustadrak Al-Wasa'el*, 12:13.

[45] Al-Harrani, *Tohaf Al-'Oqool*, 14.

[46] Al-Majlisi, *Bihar Al-Anwar*, 70:270.

[47] Al-Kulayni, *Al-Kafi*, 2:302.

Abu Thar also narrates that the Prophet (s) once said, *"If a man became angry while he is standing, let him sit down and his anger will subside. Else, let him lay down."*[48]

Constructive Anger. Not all anger is bad or prohibited. There is one type of anger that arises out of different circumstances. Anger normally arises because of satanic whispers and takes the individual outside the bounds of good conduct. Good anger, on the other hand, arises from the intellect and drives the individual towards his humanity rather than away from it. It drives the individual towards a higher and sublime understanding. It is anger that is connected to God. It is driven by devotion rather than madness. It is led by the intellect rather than ignorance. It is a force of anger that drives the individual towards reform of himself and what is around him. This type of anger is loved by God. This is the type of anger that would overcome the Prophets and righteous, as they do not become angry for this world – they only become angry for the sake of God. It is narrated that Imam Ali (a) said of the Prophet (s), *"he would not become angry for this world. But if he were to become angry for the sake of truth, he would become unrecognizable and he would not stop until he ensures that truth prevails."*[49]

It is also narrated that Prophet Moses (a) asked God, *"oh Lord, who are Your people who are in the shadow of your throne on [the Day of Judgment]? So God revealed to him:... and those who are angered by the violation of what I have made sacred, much like a tiger when wounded."*[50]

---

[48] Al-Rishahri, *Mizan Al-Hikma*, 3:2269.

[49] Ibid.

[50] Al-Amili, *Wasa'el Al-Shia*, 11:417.

It is also narrated that when Muawiyya exiled Abu Thar from the land of Sham, a number of people accompanied him until he said his farewells and advised them,

> *Oh people, combine with your prayer and your fast anger for the sake of God if He was disobeyed in this world. Do not seek the favor of your rulers through the displeasure of God. If they commit what you know to be evil, distance yourselves from them and look down upon them, even if you had to face punishment, deprivation, and exile until God in His Majesty and Glory is pleased.[51]*

The Positive Role Anger Can Play. If anger is controlled by the intellect, it can have a number of positive influences within the individual's self.

Firstly, anger plays a huge role in an individual's capability to defend, not only himself, but his family, wealth, nation, and religion as well. Anger gives rise to fervor and devotion that drive us to protect our families and our faith. Through the force of anger, an individual may be able to attain some of the highest honors. Without it, you would not be able to attain the honor of defending your family or your country, or the higher honor of defending your faith. However, anger does not know the difference between *halal* and *haram*. It does not know boundaries and it cannot determine the right way to act. If it is not controlled, it is only goal is to destroy. That is why it must be strictly controlled by the intellect. The intellect is the tool that is able to transform it from a blind and reckless force to a disciplined and orderly passion. That is why God has set strict guidance on reclaiming your

---

51 Al-Mufid, *Al-Amali*, 163.

rights. He says, "*So should anyone aggress against you, assail him in the manner he assailed you, and be wary of God, and know that God is with the God-wary.*"[52]

Secondly, anger can be used as a passion to balance the passion of desires. Desires are unique in that they are stubborn and persistent. Hunger and sexual drive are insistent issues that may cause the intellect to lose control at times. Even some believers might at times lose control and succumb to the power of desires to fall into sin. Some might find themselves powerless against these desires. Here comes the role of anger that is unique in its intensity and how quickly it can calm down. That is why scholars of ethics emphasize the use of anger as a means to counteract desires. When a person's fervor and devotion are used to counter his regressive desires, he will be able to quell them quickly. As Plato once said, "How difficult is it for a person who is entrenched in desires to be virtuous? A person who i thought and desires do not prefer balance must seek the aid of the force of anger that gives rise to fervor and devotion to overcome the desires."[53]

Thirdly, anger can be used to reach a number of noble characteristics. Anyone who is able to use the force of anger to quell his desires will have taken a great step towards self-purification. Similarly, a person who uses the force of anger to defend his honor, wealth, family, nation, or faith will have reached a great status of noble character. On the other hand, someone standing up to the negative implications of this force and containing his wrath reaches a great status

[52] The Holy Quran, Chapter 2 [The Cow; Arabic: *Al-Baqara*], Verse 194.
[53] Al-Naraqi, *Jami' Al-Sa'adat*, 1:62.

and will have attained plentiful rewards and a close position to God. This is what our Imams (a) tell us in their narrations. Imam Baqir (a) is narrated to have said, *"whoever is able to contain his rage when he was in a position to unleash it, God will fill his heart with faith and security on the Day of Judgment."*[54] It is also narrated that Imam Sadiq (a) said, *"there is no dose that can be swallowed by a servant more beloved to God than a dose of anger; a man would swallow it due to benevolence or patience as it hangs in his heart."*[55]

Illusion

The scholars of ethics have defined the faculty of illusion as "the force that derives all sorts of ploys, ruses, and other means to reach a goal through fraud and trickery."[56]

This faculty has a great danger within the human self, as it is the faculty that may drive an individual to find all sorts of tricks to reach an end. It is not able to distinguish between truth and falsehood or between good and evil. It only wishes to reach its goals – "the end justifies the means." And so illusion is regarded as a dangerous tendency within the human self, as it can be a double-edged sword that can be used for either good or evil. If it becomes controlled by anger, the individual becomes a tyrant who attempts to reach his personal goals and satisfaction by means of corruption and tyranny. He will use illusion and deception for his personal gains. If this force falls under the control of the desires, we will see the individual scheming to satisfy his desires by any means possible.

---

54 Al-Kulayni, *Al-Kafi*, 2:110.
55 Ibid. 2:111.
56 Al-Naraqi, *Jami' Al-Sa'adat*, 1:62.

Many people think that using this faculty to get what you want is just the smart thing to do. In fact, the Quran has been clear in its warnings against the dangers of illusion, and that its improper use will only result in harm for the person misusing it. It may allow a person to reach his goals in the short run, but truth will quickly appear and people will see through the illusion. Only what is right will remain; as the Holy Quran says:

> *They had sworn by God with solemn oaths that if a warner were to come to them, they would be better guided than any of the nations. But when a warner came to them, it only increased their distance [from the truth], due to their domineering [conduct] in the land and their devising of evil schemes; and evil schemes beset only their authors. So do they await anything except the precedent of the ancients? Yet you will never find any change in God's precedent, and you will never find any revision in God's precedent.[57]*

It is also narrated that the Commander of the Faithful (a) said, *"whoever deceives others, God will turn his deception against him."*[58]

Some may, due to their misperceptions, try to apply a false standard to The Commander of the Faithful (a) and Muawiyya. They would say that Muawiyya was a cunning politician who was able to reach what he sought, while The Commander of the Faithful (a) did not have this characteristic. Anyone who draws such a comparison is trying to condemn The Commander of the Faithful (a) but is not able to do so – rather he has only praised him. True, The Com-

---

[57] The Holy Quran, Chapter 35 [The Originator; Arabic: *Fatir*], Verses 42, 43.
[58] Al-Wasiti, *'Uyoon Al-Hikam wal Mawa'ez*, 435.

mander of the Faithful (a) will never practice acts that were forbidden by God in the Holy Quran, or those that the Prophet (s) warned against. How could Imam Ali (a) practice trickery and deception for the sake of this fleeting world? Yet he himself proclaims that Muawiyya's ways are no secret to him, and that Muawiyya is not more cunning than him. He says:

> By God, Muawiyya is not more cunning than I am. He betrays and corrupts. If treachery was no vice, I would have been the most cunning of men. But every betrayal is a corruption and every corruption is disbelief. Each traitor carries a banner that identifies him on the Day of Judgment. God is not tricked by deception nor is he overpowered with force.[59]

The Prophet (s) and the Immaculates (a) have emphasized that deception will always revert back and harm whoever practices it. In essence, whoever practices deception is challenging God to undo his schemes. And so God will deal with him with His cunning – "*they plot and God devises, and God is the best of devisers.*"[60] God also says in the Holy Quran, "*They devised a plot, and We [too] devised a plan, but they were not aware. So observe how was the outcome of their plotting, as We destroyed them and all their people.*"[61]

Cunning is not Inherently Evil. Cunning is not an inherently evil characteristic. It is a vice when it is controlled by desires or by anger, such that it only plans towards sin. However, if cunning is under the control of the intellect and

59 Al-Radi, Nahj *Al-Balagha*, 2:180, Sermon 200.
60 The Holy Quran, Chapter 8 [The Spoils of War; Arabic: *Al-Anfal*], Verse 30.
61 The Holy Quran, Chapter 27 [The Ants; Arabic: *Al-Naml*], Verses 50, 51.

is used for good and virtue, it would be a praiseworthy characteristic. And we see that God describes Himself as the best of devisers in the Holy Quran because His cunning is aimed towards the best outcomes and through correct means. So whenever a man uses his cunning to reach closer to perfection through legitimate means, to reach a higher status and closeness to God, this cunning becomes a force for God and a soldier of the intellect. Conversely, if cunning is used to attain the fleeting pleasures of this world and to oppress others, it becomes a vice that only brings evil towards the individual.

It is important to point out that cunning is a powerful force within the human self. Through it, an individual can plan and manage the affairs of his life and attain whatever he needs for a decent life, assuming that he does not overstep the bounds of religion and morality. If we were not able to use this faculty, we would have been an easy prey for the simplest of beings and we would not have been able to manage our lives.

Believer Beware. The believer must not be envious of the deceitful who is able to get what he wants through trickery. These momentary gains will fade away soon. Even if they last for years on this Earth, that is nothing compared to the eternity of the hereafter. What riches was Muawiyya able to reap through his trickery? Where has it all gone now? Where is he now? How can we compare the few years of worldly pleasure to the eternity of hellfire?

On the other hand, the Commander of the Faithful lives in an eternity of grace. His remembrance lives on and will continue to live on. He lives on because he preferred truth over all else. He followed the commands and words of God rather than the way of deception.

A believer must be of utmost caution of God's cunning. How many times does God give a person the bounties and blessings of this world, only to have that person fall into the trap of the love for this world? Whenever we receive a blessing, we must beware not to fall into that trap.

Imam Ali (a) said, "*Oh people, let God see you afraid of his blessings, much like you are averse to his wrath. Whoever is blessed with plenty and did not see that as a bait, he has fallen into [false] security while danger is overhead.*"[62] It is also narrated that Imam Sadiq (a) said, "*if you see a person searching for the defects in others and forgetting his own defects, know that he has been deceived.*"[63]

Not every blessing that a person receives is truly a blessing; some may be a trap in disguise. We must beware of these traps at times of contentment even more than at times of trials and tribulations. In times of trials and tribulations, the test should be clear. In times of contentment, the blessings themselves may be trials in disguise.

A person may busy himself with searching for defects in others with disregard for his own defects. A person may judge everyone but himself. A person may begin placing people in heaven and hell in accordance with his desires, without looking at himself and his defects. That is a sign that the person has fallen into a trap and failed a divine test.

Whatever genius and cunning an individual may have, he will not be able to outsmart God. The only way to avoid

---

[62] Al-Radi, *Nahj Al-Balagha*, 4:83, Saying 358.
[63] Al-Harrani, *Tohaf Al-'Oqool*, 364.

God's cunning is through his mercy. We ask God to have mercy on us by not devising traps where we may unwittingly fall. Therefore, it is important to always beware of God's cunning and ask him for his mercy. God wants the best for us. He is not out to get us. But we give ourselves the short end of the stick when we turn away from God.

THE BATTLE

The faculties within the human self are all blessings from God. Without them, we would not have been able to live out our lives, let alone move closer to God on the path of perfection. However, each of these faculties has its own motives and it seeks to attain them by any means.

The desires seek to fulfill their hunger and lust. Whenever the desires take control over a person, he becomes like cattle with no worry other than food and drink – *"They are just like cattle; indeed, they are further astray from the way."*[64] Imam Ali (a) says of such people, *"whoever takes as his sole concern what enters his stomach, his worth is equal to what is excreted by it."*[65]

Anger seeks to attack, harm, and destroy whatever stands in its way. If anger controls a person, he becomes a wild and bloodthirsty beast. If anger takes hold, people become willing to kill even the prophets and the righteous. God says:

> *Certainly, We gave Moses the Book and followed him with the apostles, and We gave Jesus, the son of Mary, manifest proofs and confirmed him with the Holy Spirit. Is it not that whenever an apostle brought you that which was not to*

---

[64] The Holy Quran, Chapter 25 [Arabic: *Al-Furqan*], Verse 44.
[65] Al-Wasiti, *'Uyoon Al-Hikam wal Mawa'ez*, 436.

*your liking, you would act arrogantly; so you would impugn
a group [of them], and slay [another] group?*[66]

God also says, *"Say, 'Then why would you kill the prophets of God
formerly, should you be faithful?"*[67] Such a person will bring corruption to the Earth and will be worse than the beasts, as he has other faculties to aid his anger.

The faculty of illusion seeks to devise plans and can deceive others. If it gains control over a person, he becomes a satanic being. The Quran has described these people as devils:

*That is how for every prophet We appointed as enemy the
devils from among humans and jinn, who inspire each other
with flashy words, deceptively. Had your Lord wished, they
would not have done it. So leave them with what they fabricate.*[68]

The goal of the intellect is to control the other faculties within the human self. The intellect is what drives the individual closer towards purity and closeness to God. The intellect is thus a force for the divine as long as it remains in control of the other faculties. However, if it falls under the control of any of the other faculties, it loses its benevolent characteristic – the intellect in that state transforms into ignorance.

Each of these faculties that exist within the human self seeks its own satisfaction and fulfilment. They are competing and battling amongst themselves, and each of them has its soldiers in this battle. Scholars of ethics have character-

---

66 The Holy Quran, Chapter 2 [The Cow; Arabic: *Al-Baqara*], Verse 87.
67 Ibid. Verse 91.
68 The Holy Quran, Chapter 6 [The Cattle; Arabic: *Al-An'am*], Verse 112.

ized the battle as such: "God has given the intellect its soldiers, and allowed the other faculties to make use of the soldiers of ignorance and Satan. The battle that takes place is thus a battle between the soldiers of God the Merciful and the soldiers of Satan. This battle is described as the Greater Struggle."[69]

THE SUPPORT LINES

The role of the intellect is to control the other faculties, to create balance between them, and to drive them on the path of excellence towards God. But will intellect be able to claim victory in this battle without the assistance of a Divine Legislator?

The intellect and religious teachings can be likened to the road and the source of light for the wayfarer. For a person to reach his destination, he has to have a path to walk, as well as a source of light that will allow him to see the path. The intellect is the light source and religious teachings are the path. I cannot reach my destination without having the two of them. The intellect lights the way by controlling the faculties and leading them on the path. But the intellect cannot lead if it does not know the path. God, therefore, draws the path for us through His means of guidance – the Quran, the Prophet (s), and the Holy Household (a) – so that the intellect can lead the faculties to the ultimate goal. In a sermon about the intellect and its role, Imam Sadiq (a) explained:

---

[69] Al-Haidari, *Al-Tarbiya Al-Roohiyya*, 173.

If he was told "does the intellect suffice the servants so that they are not in need for anything else?" He would say "a person who is cognizant of the indications of his intellect — which has been given to him by God as a strong foundation, an adornment, and a guide — would know that God is the Truth and that God is his Lord. He would know that his creator has a capacity to love and hate, and that He has [commands that can be met with] obedience or disobedience. Yet, his intellect could not lead him to that [detailed code of commands]. He would know that he would not reach it by any means other than seeking knowing, and that his intellect cannot aid him in this endeavor without knowledge. Therefore, it became an obligation on the person of intellect to seek the knowledge and education without which he would have no strong foundation."[70]

The intellect realizes that there are obligations that the creator has ordained and that there are things that the creator dislikes. However, the intellect alone cannot discover all these limits. Therefore, there must be a guide that draws all these boundaries and gives the intellect a path where it can lead the individual. The intellect also plays a role in discovering the defects and distortions that may exist in any proposed path — because, as we know, there have been many who have tried to distort the message of the Prophet (a) and to misrepresent his teachings.

Each faculty of the human self tries to achieve its own goals, despite the chaos and corruption that it might cause. Therefore, there must be a set of laws that bind these faculties and draw boundaries for their actions. The intellect

---

[70] Al-Kulayni, *Al-Kafi*, 1:29, Tr. 34.

alone cannot put all this in place – it can control and limit the faculties, but it lacks detailed laws concerning when to bind them. So there must be a set of laws that draws the boundaries for the faculties and their proper use.

In this great battle, the intellect faces a great opponent. At times, the intellect may be defeated without knowing that it was defeated. If the intellect falls under the control of one of the other faculties, and becomes captive to them rather than being their leader, it has faced a great defeat. It may fall victim to the faculties and work solely to serve them without even realizing it. God says, *"Say, 'Shall we inform you who are the biggest losers in their works? Those whose efforts are misguided in the life of the world, while they suppose they are doing good.'"*[71]

The role of religion in this process is as a measure for the intellect's ability to remain steadfast on the path or deviation away from it. The Commander of the Faithful describes the role of the Prophets as showing the path that the intellect must take – he says:

> *From [Adam's] progeny God chose prophets and took their pledge for his revelation and for carrying His message as their trust. In course of time many people perverted God's trust with them and ignored His position and took compeers along with Him. Satan turned them away from knowing Him and kept them aloof from His worship. Then God sent His Messengers and series of His prophets towards them to get them to fulfil the pledges of His creation, to re-call to them His bounties, to exhort them by preaching, to*

---

[71] The Holy Quran. Chapter 18 [The Cave; Arabic: *Al-Kahf*]. Verses 103, 104.

unveil before them the hidden virtues of the intellect and show them the signs of His Omnipotence[72]

We should point out here the importance of having an immaculate guide at all times. The battle within the human self does not stop – it has been ongoing in every human since the time of Prophet Adam (a) until today. And since the intellect alone is not enough to reach the ultimate goal that God desires for us, there must be a guide at all times that supports the intellect. This is not restricted to the time of the prophets and the messengers, but extends to our time as well. It is also not limited to matters of delivering Divine law, but encompasses channeling Divine mercy to us from God. Therefore, an immaculate guide must at all times be present on the Earth to be God's proof over his creations and their guide towards God's path. We believe that this guide today is the Twelfth Imam from Ahlulbayt (a). There is no problem that our Immaculate Imam (a) is in occultation at the moment, as his role does not require an apparent identity that people can recognize openly. We may not be able to benefit from him by direct physical access, but we believe that he delivers his graces to us through his many means. The Immaculate Imams (a) have put in place the mechanisms that allow us to follow on their path and safeguard our communities from deviance. The system of Twelver Shia Islamic law, expertly deduced by our upright jurists, sprouts from the teachings of the immaculate guides. Moreover, it is reported that Prophet Muhammad (saws) described how people would benefit from the hidden Imam

---

[72] Al-Radi, *Nahj Al-Balagha*, 1:23, Sermon 1.

just as the earth benefits from the sun even when clouds conceal it.[73]

DISCIPLINING THE TROOPS

One of the great blessings of God – alongside the blessing of the intellect – is that of a perfect system of worship that plays a significant role in disciplining the faculties within the human self. As we mentioned earlier, these faculties play an essential role in the struggle within as they become troops controlled by whichever side that comes to control them. We will point out a number of important points in this regard:

Firstly, the Holy Quran references the role of worship in disciplining the self and achieving a state of piety – God says: *"Recite what has been revealed to you of the Book, and maintain the prayer. Indeed the prayer restrains from indecent and wrongful conduct, and the remembrance of God is surely greater. And God knows whatever [deeds] you do."*[74] The role of prayer is to reduce the excesses that a person may fall into and guide him back to the path of God. God also clarifies the role of fasting – *"O you who have faith! Prescribed for you is fasting as it was prescribed for those who were before you, so that you may be God-wary."*[75] Thus, fasting creates a level of God-wariness that allows the individual to control his faculties and safeguard them from falling into sin. And there are many verses that carry similar meanings.

---

[73] Al-Saduq, *Ikmal al-Din*, 1:253

[74] The Holy Quran, Chapter 29 [The Spider; Arabic: *Al-Ankaboot*], Verse 45.

[75] The Holy Quran, Chapter 2 [The Cow; Arabic: *Al-Baqara*], Verse 183.

We can clearly see the role of worship in disciplining the self when we see its effect on our selves. We find that when we fast and refrain from food, drink, and sexual activity, we train our desires to become used to limitations in this sense. I discipline myself by not giving it what it wants; so it knows that it cannot have whatever it desires. The Immaculates (a) have emphasized this dimension of fasting – that it is not simply refraining from food and drink. Fasting draws the boundaries for all of the faculties of the human self. Imam Sadiq (a) is narrated to have said, *"fasting is not from food and drink so that a man simply does not eat or drink. Rather, if you fast let your hearing, sight, tongue, stomach, and privates all fast. Safeguard your hands and privates, and prolong your silence...."*[76]

Through this great worship, a person is able to tame and control the self that strays towards evil. It trains the faculties of the self to be disciplined, in addition to purifying the soul of any sins and transgressions. Refraining from food and drink and safeguarding the faculties create a state of purity and enlightenment in the heart. That strengthens the intellect and allows it to take control and leadership of the faculties.

Worship also strengthens the social fabric through creating an environment that builds stronger bonds between members of the community. As we engage in communal worship, we collectively move closer to God. Group prayers and fasting during the Holy Month of Ramadhan, for example, play an essential role in strengthening the bond of brotherhood between mankind. All this has the effect of having love and harmony pervade the community. This will

---

[76] Al-Amili, *Wasa'el Al-Shia*, 7:118.

limit the power of anger and deception through the sense of God-wariness. This will transform these faculties from ones that are working to undermine the individual's development to ones that are guided by the intellect to serve his development.

BENEVOLENCE

In the name of God, the most Beneficent, the most Merciful

Indeed God enjoins justice and kindness, and generosity towards relatives, and He forbids indecency, wrongdoing, and aggression. He advises you, so that you may take admonition.[1]

The foundation of a solid and upright life was not solely built on the acts of worship. Though some forms of worship, like prayer and fasting, have their grace, virtue, and great role in bringing one closer to God, they are not the only tools that a person has to better his relationship with God. Likewise, they are not the only tools that can be used to build a tight virtuous community where a person can be closer to God. In much of the teachings of Ahlulbayt (a), we notice pointers to other types of activities that a person should practice in order to complete his faith. Thus, simply performing the acts of worship does not render a person religious, or committed to his faith. There are many people who are wanton and immoral but are committed to superficial acts of worship like prayer and fasting. Does that mean

---

[1] The Holy Quran. Chapter 16 [The Bees; Arabic: *Al-Nahl*]. Verse 90.

that they are actually benefiting from those prayers and fasting? The Commander of the Faithful (a) said:

> How many people fast and do not gain anything from their fasting except hunger and thirst? And how many people rise [for their prayer] and do not gain anything from that but lack of rest and fuss. The sleep, as well as the eating and drinking, of the intelligent (God-conscious) person is far better.[2]

The Imams of Ahlulbayt (a) provided us with the guidance to identify what it means to be people of the religion, beyond superficial acts of worship. Imam Ali (a) said

> The people of religion have signs that they can be identified with: truth in their conversation, holding trusts, fulfilling their promises, keeping family ties, being merciful to the weak, lack of over indulgence in sexual activity, enjoining the good, positive temperament, upright character, and following knowledge that will bring one closer to God – blessed they are and blessed be their final destination.[3]

Many of us assess others' religiosity based on their performance and participation in acts of worship. As soon as we see one of these people do something in disagreement with religion, we hold all religious people accountable for that person's mistake. This is really unfortunate, because the initial assessment was wrong. Religion is not the external form of worship alone. Religion is worship, societal interaction, ethics and morals, organization and administration of social, economic, and political affairs, amongst other things.

---

[2] Al-Radi, *Nahj Al-Balagha*, 4:35, Tr. 145
[3] Al-Majlisi, *Bihar Al-Anwar*, 4:35, Tr. 145.

A religious person is one who commits to the guidelines of religious law in every aspect, he does not pick and choose out of convenience. This is what differentiates Islam from other religions and ideologies. Islam does not accept such discrimination, whereby a person commits to some aspects of the faith without the rest of its parts. Rather, Islam has reproached this type of lack of commitment as shown in the following verse:

> *Then there you were, killing your folks and expelling a part of your folks from their homes, backing one another against them in sin and aggression! And if they came to you as captives, you would ransom them, though their expulsion itself was forbidden you. What! Do you believe in part of the Book and deny another part? So what is the requital of those of you who do that except disgrace in the life of this world? And on the Day of Resurrection, they shall be consigned to the severest punishment. And God is not oblivious of what you do.*[4]

To not commit to the worships as God has ordained is considered to be transgressing the limits he has placed. Likewise, lack of commitment to proper dealing and conduct is considered to be transgressing those same limits. Regarding such limits, on the matter of the time of fasting God said:

> *You are permitted on the night of the fast to go into your wives: they are a garment for you, and you are a garment for them. God knew that you would betray yourselves, so He pardoned you and excused you. So now consort with them and seek what God has ordained for you, and eat and*

---

[4] The Holy Quran. Chapter 2 [The Cow; Arabic: *Al-Baqara*]. Verse 85.

drink until the white streak becomes manifest to you from the dark streak at the crack of dawn. Then complete the fast until nightfall, and do not consort with them while you dwell in confinement in the mosques. These are God's bounds, so do not approach them. Thus does God clarify His signs for mankind so that they may be Godwary.[5]

On the matter of divorce and the rights of the spouse:

[Revocable] divorce may be only twice; then [let there be] either an honorable retention, or a kindly release. It is not lawful for you to take back anything from what you have given them, unless the couple fear that they may not maintain God's bounds; so if you fear they would not maintain God's bounds, there is no sin upon them in what she may give to secure her own release. These are God's bounds, so do not transgress them, and whoever transgresses the bounds of God—it is they who are the wrongdoers.[6]

This is a clear proof that God sees religion as a whole not to be partitioned. There are matters that are considered essential in religion, and that is not merely superficial worship. Rather, in reality every commitment to the commands of God is worship and servitude. Of course, trying one's best to commit to faith is better than not committing to faith at all. Facing challenges with commitment does not warrant abandoning commitment altogether. But the emphasis should be aimed at progress toward genuine, holistic commitment to God's spiritual prescription for us. That is how the prescription can do its job and how we can please God.

---

[5] Ibid. Verse 187.
[6] Ibid. Verse 229.

God has provided a significant concept in the life of a believer, and that is the concept of benevolence, or 'doing good.' This concept is very broad and encompasses a number of meanings. Still, we can say that in this context of ethics it relates to all the aspects of religious commitments: worship, social interactions, and transactions.

THE MEANING OF DOING GOOD

From both the Holy Quran and the noble narrations we find that doing good has a broad understanding that encompasses many meanings.

One meaning is perfection in one's work and intention, as evidenced by a narration from Omar bin Yazid who said, "I heard Aba Abdillah (a) say, *'If a believer perfects his work, God will reward his deeds by 700 times…'*"[7]

Another meaning comes as sincerity of intention toward God in all our work, and fearing Him as a result of being aware of His watching over what we do. The explanation of what it means to do good has been given by the Prophet (s) in his explanation of the following verse: "*Yet excuse them and forbear. Indeed God loves the virtuous.*"[8] He explained that the meaning of doing good is, "*to worship God as if you see Him; and if you cannot see Him, he sees you.*"[9]

A third meaning of 'doing good' refers to any and every good deed a person does. In many verses of the Holy Quran, God follows the mentioning of a good deed carried

---

[7] Al-Huwayzi, *Noor Al-Thaqalayn*, 1:181.

[8] The Holy Quran. Chapter 2 [The Cow; Arabic: *Al-Baqara*]. Verse 112.

[9] Al-Huwayzi, *Noor Al-Thaqalay*, 1:553.

out by a human being with, "God loves the good-doers."
An example of this is: *"... so pardon them and turn away; surely
God loves those who do good (to others)."*[10] Also, when He said,
*"...then they are careful (of their duty) and do good (to others), and
God loves those who do good (to others)."*[11] This is the case in
dozens of other verses. A good-doer is one who practices
benevolence – who does 'good.' Thus, every good deed and
righteous action is looked at by God as benevolence, or 'doing good,' and the person who carries out the action is
good-doer.

A fourth meaning of doing good is specifically mentioned as
doing good onto others without reciprocity. This person
meets good with what is greater, and meets evil with what is
lesser. He does good onto others voluntarily without good
being done to him first.[12]

There are numerous narrations that indicate God's command to do good and its necessity. In the following verse,
God makes this clear: *"Indeed God enjoins justice and kindness,
and generosity towards relatives, and He forbids indecency, wrongdoing,
and aggression. He advises you, so that you may take admonition."*[13]

Doing good equates to justice and giving to the near of kin.
We know the importance of justice, given its station as one
of the pillars of faith and stems from the oneness of God.
Imagine how important justice is when it is Divine Justice
that explains the need for matters as important as Divine
Judgment and Prophet-hood. A sound mind sees that jus-

---

[10] The Holy Quran. Chapter 5 [The Spread; Arabic: *Al-Maeda*] Verse 13.

[11] Ibid. Verse 93.

[12] Al-Tabatabaei, *Tafsir Al-Mizan*, 12:332.

[13] The Holy Quran. Chapter 16 [The Bees; Arabic: *Al-Nahl*]. Verse 90.

tice should be done. This is because justice is good. And why should good be done? That is self-evident. Doing good is a worthy goal in and of itself. But doing good also has practical benefits similar to how justice has practical benefits. Justice is important in building, advancing and safeguarding society, and so is doing good. This will become clearer when we discuss the role of doing good in safeguarding society.

Through the mentioned meanings of benevolence, it becomes clear that doing good is the ethical aspect that relates to all types of religious commitments. This is regarding worship-related activities, social transactions, and the general relationship between the individual and God. It is also related to the relationship between individuals themselves, regarding their dealings with one another, their rights and obligations. Moreover, it is connected to humanitarian matters like lifting oppression from the weak, aiding the poor, pardoning wrongdoers and other related issues.

THE IMPORTANCE OF DOING GOOD

Some propose the following idea: God sent down His law, His Holy Book, and the teachings of His Greatest Prophet (s) – everything needed to provide order to the affairs of humanity. He made clear the limitations of the acceptable and the prohibited, and what was obligated and what was not. Is adhering to these guidelines enough to establish a godly society ruled by virtues in all sense of the word? Another way of posing the question, is it possible to establish a society based on law and not based on benevolence?

To answer these questions, we say the following:

It is not possible to build a complete and happy society based solely on law – as in the "limitations" as described in religious law. The law shows us our rights and obligations. The scholars of law say, "the eyes of justice are blind," illustrating that they do not see beyond facts and rights; and thus, they give each his due right. This is extremely important in building and maintaining a righteous and stable society. If law did not exist, people would have transgressed against each other and societies would turn into hotbeds of tension and endless fighting grounds that will not end except with corruption and ruin. Law has a huge role in safeguarding society. Nonetheless, is the law alone enough? The Islamic vision to safeguarding society calls to linking the law with benevolence. Islam is perhaps the only system in today's age that links the two. It makes clear the rights of each individual, while calling on people to do good. This is not only in situations of conflict but in every aspect of life. Here are some examples:

Benevolence in Marriage

Much importance is placed on family in Islam. The family unit is essential to building a righteous society. Each family member's rights and obligations are known and identified in Islam. However, the religion did not commit people simply to the limitations of rights and obligations in the family unit; rather, it called for acting on mercy and love. *"And of His signs is that He created for you mates from your own selves that you may take comfort in them, and He ordained affection and mercy between you. There are indeed signs in that for a people who reflect."*[14]

---

[14] The Holy Quran. Chapter 30 [The Romans; Arabic: *Al-Room*]. Verse 21.

In addition, the Holy Prophet (s) and Ahlulbayt (a) have made clear statements as to the rights of both husband and wife. However, we notice that there is a repeated call to benevolence and doing good toward one another. There are many narrations that encourage the husband and father to treat his wife and family with benevolence, respectively. Even in times of dispute we notice that the religious legislator makes clear who is in the right, but at the same time the legislator calls for commitment to ethics and morality in action. The wisdom behind some rulings goes back to the outlook of empathy and ethics. An example of this is found in the following verse:

> *If you desire to take a wife in place of another, and you have given one of them a quintal [of gold], do not take anything away from it. Would you take it by way of calumny and flagrant sin?! How could you take it back, when you have known each other, and they have taken from you a solemn covenant?*[15]

The ruling in the above verse basically states that for a consummated marriage, whatever bridal gift you have given your wife, no matter how much, you cannot take back any of it during divorce. There is a moral lesson, a wisdom behind the ruling to be understood as one contemplates upon this verse. The relationship between husband and wife is more profound than to have the spouses deal with one another in such a way.

A clear example encouraging benevolence as opposed to strictly taking one's legal rights comes forth with the ruling

---

[15] Ibid. Verses 20 and 21.

mandating paying half of the bridal gift when the divorce involves an unconsummated marriage.

> *And if you divorce them before you touch them, and you have already settled a dowry for them, then [pay them] half of what you have settled, unless they forgo it, or someone in whose hand is the marriage tie forgoes it. And to forgo is nearer to Godwariness; so do not forget graciousness among yourselves. Indeed God watches what you do.*[16]

Here, God shows the rights of each spouse and the religious restrictions placed in such a case. However, he concludes the verse by stating that it is better to forgive, let go, and not forget the virtue and favor between you.

Islam makes clear the limitations and restrictions, but it goes further and raises the bar to have people commit to more than just meeting basic standards or limits. That extra push is benevolence – doing good to one another – which plays a tremendous role in bringing the members of a family closer to each other. Family life is not a job. We are not employees that clock in and clock out when we are done with our shift. That is not the way family life works. We have to feel, be empathetic, and treat others with goodness. When we do that we can make it through family life with the accompanying struggles, pain, and hardships.

Benevolence with Parents

What is most interesting about our relationship with our parents, in the context of this discussion, is that it differs from many relationships in their framework of responsibility and religious restrictions. The ethical sentiment in the

---

[16] The Holy Quran. Chapter 2 [The Cow; Arabic: *Al-Baqara*]. Verse 237.

relationship between parent and child is found in this verse: *"Your Lord has decreed that you shall not worship anyone except Him, and [He has enjoined] kindness to parents."*[17] This moral sentiment in dealing with our parents is not limited to religious rights and obligations of the parent versus the child or the like. Rather, what is expected in this relationship is to give benevolently – financially, emotionally, and in service. While benevolence is encouraged in other relationships, there is a special emphasis on benevolence in one's relationship with his/her parents. *"Lower the wing of humility to them, mercifully, and say: My Lord! Have mercy on them, just as they reared me when I was [a] small [child]!"*[18]

I ask: is there a law in this world related to the parent-child relationship (rights, obligations, etc.) that is founded on benevolence? Current positive laws (i.e. man-made laws) have relied on the lessons derived from the human experience. The greatest legal theorists, who have derived those laws, have not been able to find a solution for the worsening social problem of the breakdown of family structure. This is especially true when such family structures are built solely on a legal basis. Whenever they tried to close a gap in the laws, they find many other gaps open in return. So even with all the advancements and great experiences that mankind has seen on Earth, we are still incapable of creating laws that are harmonious with humanity. Islam, however, has promoted a different sentiment in relationships between children and their parents - it is that of benevolence.

---

[17] The Holy Quran. Chapter 17[The Ascension; Arabic: *Al-Israa*]. Verse 23.
[18] Ibid. Verse 24.

Benevolence in Relationships

It is clear to us from our Islamic teachings, that with all the rights, responsibilities and obligations we have towards people, God has always called on us to do good onto others. We can see that in the following areas:

Disputes. When people are in an adversarial state or in a dispute of some sort, the slogan "reconciliation is better" is raised. Each should be given his due right – falling suit with the religious limitations and each is entitled to his full right. Still, God encourages us to loosen our hold on our rights in order to accomplish that reconciliation.

> *The well-off and the opulent among you should not vow that they will not give [any longer] to the relatives and the needy, and to those who have migrated in the way of God, and let them excuse and forbear. Do you not love that God should forgive you? God is all-forgiving, all-merciful.*[19]

This verse points to the reality that we must treat one another with benevolence and goodness, before we expect God to treat us with His forgiveness as opposed to his firm justice. Who of us would be able to enter paradise if God wished to treat us on the basis of His justice, not on the basis of His generosity, and mercy? So long as we are in need of God's benevolence and generosity, we should behave in line with God's etiquettes and treat others within the framework of goodness. This is all in regards to disputes, arguments, and demanding rights.

How to Interact with Enemies. In regards to the administration of society we rarely find a piece of legislation that

---

[19] The Holy Quran. Chapter 24 [The Light; Arabic: *Al-Noor*]. Verse 22.

calls for benevolence toward all members of society in all of their diversity. Such goodness is not intended exclusively for one religious group over others. Do you know of a religion that calls its people to be friendly towards their enemies? *"Good and evil [conduct] are not equal. Repel [evil] with what is best. [If you do so,] he between whom and you was enmity, will then be as though he were a sympathetic friend."*[20]

Civic Relationships. In the matter of governance, Islam gives citizens who do not believe in the faith the same rights enjoyed by those who are considered followers of the governor and his faith. Islam promotes the outlook that people are equal in creation and mercy is mandatory across all members of society, regardless whether or not they are Muslim. The Commander of the Faithful (a) advised his governor of Egypt, Malik Al-Ashtar the following:

> *Habituate your heart to mercy for the subjects and to affection and kindness for them. Do not stand over them like greedy beasts who feel it is enough to devour them, since they are of two kinds, either your brother in religion or one like you in creation... So, extend to them your forgiveness and pardon, in the same way as you would like God to extend His forgiveness and pardon to you.*[21]

Dealing with One Another. The Holy Quran is very straightforward with regards to doing good to others. In one verse, referring to a particular group of those of different faiths, the Quran says:

---

[20] The Holy Quran. Chapter 41 [Arabic: *Fussilat*]. Verse 34.
[21] Al-Radi, Nahj Al-Balagha, 3:84, Letter 53.

God does not forbid you from dealing with kindness and justice with those [polytheists] who did not make war against you on account of religion and did not expel you from your homes. Indeed God loves the just.[22]

If God orders us to behave in such a way with people of another faith, then how should we interact with our fellow believers and amongst ourselves? Thus, there is no doubt that benevolence is what we should intend and strive to realize in our lives. We should strive for doing good not just to uphold rights and obligations, but to bring to life true happiness and the advancement of our society. Those things will only come to fruition with benevolence and goodness. And ultimately, we should be benevolent because that is a worthy goal in and of itself. God is with the person who does good as he says, *"Indeed God is with those who are Godwary and those who are virtuous."*[23] God also mentions in another verse, *"As for those who strive in Us, We shall surely guide them in Our ways, and God is indeed with the virtuous."*[24] And how can one not be comforted and advance forward when God is by his side.

---

[22] The Holy Quran. Chapter 60 [Arabic: *Al-Mumtahana*]. Verse 8.

[23] The Holy Quran. Chapter 16 [The Bees; Arabic: *Al-Nahl*]. Verse 128.

[24] The Holy Quran. Chapter 29 [The Spider; Arabic: *Al-Ankabout*]. Verse 69.

THE LITTLE TIME WE HAVE

In the name of God, the most Beneficent, the most Merciful

Did We not open your breast for you and relieve you of your burden which [almost] broke your back? Did We not exalt your name? Indeed ease accompanies hardship. Indeed ease accompanies hardship. So when you are done, appoint, and supplicate your Lord.[1]

This amazing chapter in the Quran, though very short, contains some very important studies of knowledge – specifically in essential matters of theology. We are particularly interested in what is mentioned in the verses *"So when you are done, appoint, and supplicate your Lord."[2]* These two verses point to a significant meaning and a reality to which we must pay attention, and that is the issue of 'free-time' and how to benefit from the time we have in our lives without wasting it. If we are to look at our reality, we would find that no matter how many years we live, they will only account to a few simple moments. How fast do our days and nights pass by? Days turn to months and months turn to

---

[1] The Holy Quran. Chapter 94 [Arabic: Al-Sharh]. Verses 1-8.
[2] Ibid. Verses 7 and 8.

years, without us even feeling it. Imam Ali (a) points to this when he says, *"How fast are the hours in the day, and the days in a month, and the months in a year... and how fast the years are in a lifetime."*[3]

THE VALUE OF LIFE

We were created in this world for the purpose of being tested and tried. Each and every moment in our lives is calculated in value and recorded. God created this world as an abode for work and action, without judgment in it. But after this life, there is no work for a person to carry out. This is what is expressed by the words of the Immaculates (a) when they say that today (this world) is action and no judgment, while tomorrow is judgment and no action. This is a reality that we need to come to terms with. Another reality to understand is that no matter how high of a station we have in closeness to God, we cannot extend the length of our lives in this world. The Holy Prophet (s) said, *"... life is limited. No one will go beyond what has been ordained for him, so work before time is up."*[4]

The Commander of the Faithful (a) points to this truth when he said,

> *So, hasten towards (good) actions and dread the suddenness of death, because the return of age cannot be hoped for, as the return of livelihood can be hoped for. Whatever is missed from livelihood today may be hoped tomorrow with increase, but whatever is lost from the age yesterday, its return cannot*

---

[3] Al-Radi, *Nahj Al-Balagha*, 2:128, Sermon 188.

[4] Al-Majlisi, *Bihar Al-Anwar*, 74:179

be expected today. Hope can be only for that which is to come, while about that which is passed there is only disappointment.[5]

The conclusion that we reach here is that the happiness of the individual, and his future, are tied to what he has benefited from this life that God has given him. It is possible that an individual will not be able to understand the feeling of loss that follows not taking advantage of this life for what will benefit him in the afterlife, until he sees the actual result himself. At that moment, he will feel it because he will be living in that state of great regret.

> *Turn penitently to Him and submit to Him before the punishment overtakes you, whereupon you will not be helped. Follow the best of what has been sent down to you from your Lord, before the punishment overtakes you suddenly while you are unaware. Lest anyone should say, 'Alas for my negligence in the vicinage of God! Indeed I was among those who ridiculed.*[6]

The Holy Prophet has been narrated to have said:

> *On the Day of Judgment, twenty-four cabinets will be opened for each day of life that person lived – representing the number of hours in a day. One cabinet will be filled with light and happiness. He in turn is struck with so much joy and happiness that if such joy were to be dispersed amongst the people of hell they would be in awe distracted from the pain of the fire. That cabinet represents the hour when he was obedient to God. Then, another cabinet is*

---

5 Al-Radi, *Nahj Al-Balagha*, 1:226, Sermon 114.
6 The Holy Quran. Chapter 39 [Arabic: *Al-Zumar*]. Verses 54–56.

opened – it is dark, has a foul smell, and is horrifying. He in turn is struck with so much panic and dismay that if such dismay were to be dispersed amongst the people of heaven it would ruin their bliss. That cabinet represents the hour when he was disobedient to God. After that, the other cabinets are opened for him. He sees them empty – filled with nothing that would please or disappoint him. Those are the hours that he spent sleeping or being busy with things that were permitted (but did not hold value one way or the other). He is overcome with a feeling of sorrow and loss for the opportunities he missed. He could have filled those days with good deeds beyond description. And from this are God's words, 'it will be a day of privation [and regret]. [7] [8]

Every moment in our lives is a moment closer to our grave, getting closer to the end of our life. The time we have in our hands is a trust and a responsibility we have to uphold. All of our actions are based on time. We need to know the value of our lives and benefit from every moment in that life. We should strive to make every moment count for us and prioritize what is more important. Time is the only account we can bank on to ensure our well-being and happiness.

FREE TIME

Some people face the problem of feeling tight on time, as they try to race with time to accomplish their goals and objectives. Such a person constantly tries to use his time to his advantage and benefit from it. However, there are others

---

[7] The Holy Quran. Chapter 64 [Arabic: *Al-Taghabun*]. Verse 9.

[8] Al-Majlisi, *Bihar Al-Anwar*, 7:262.

who complain of another problem. This particular group feels they always have free-time, and do not find anything to fill their time. This is possibly one of the worst situations for a person, because such a person is simply wasting away his life. A person who complains of free-time loses himself and furthers himself away from God. Free-time is one of the things upon which God greatly frowns. A person should always have something to do, whether it be for this life or the next. The Holy Prophet (s) said, *"God looks down on the person who does not fill his time with work for this life or the after-life."*[9]

We should turn to Islam's outlook in filling one's time, whereby God has created mankind and sees that humanity should not live in a state of 'free-time,' which translates to time-wasting. A person should live his life in a way where he is striving toward God, moving from one struggle to another and overcoming them. There should not be wasted time so that God would frown upon this person. The following verse is clear that when a person goes through a trial and tribulation, after passing such a trial one should continue to busy himself with worship and work: *"So when you are done, appoint, and supplicate your Lord."*[10] Thus, the way of God is that of work, dedication, and effort. Here it is important to note some comments on this subject:

Free Time Corrupts the Individual

Free-time, or not using one's time, plays a big role in per-verting the individual. Free-time brings people closer to fan-

---

[9] Ibn Abi Al-Hadeed, *Sharh Nahj Al-Balagha*, 17:146.
[10] The Holy Quran. Chapter 94 [Arabic: Al-Sharh]. Verses 7 and 8.

tasizing and what is associated behaviors, in that he becomes detached from reality. Imam Ali (a) describes this when he says, *"From free-time comes boyishness."*[11] The Imam (a) here is referring to the ignorance of youthfulness and the heedlessness that comes with it. Even a balanced person can fall into this in the state of free-time. If he was busy instead, he would not find himself falling into ignorant playfulness and boyishness. Another narration from Imam Ali (a) points to this: *"If work is stressful, then in the same way, free-time is corruptive."*[12]

We feel uptight when we are bored and are not filling our time with what will benefit us. Thus, it is a natural inclination for us to strive to fill our time, to work, and to busy ourselves. A person will fill his time with things that will benefit him or things that would harm him, or at least will not bring him benefit. There are negative consequences to filling his time and they will affect him either directly in this life or in the afterlife. This is important to remember.

Where is Free Time in the Divine Plan?

In some societies and cultures, there are long periods of time off given to people – especially the youth and teenagers. In this time a lot of experimentation with the wrong things can take place. On a general level, youth, teenagers, and students find themselves with a lot of time on their hands. A specific example of this is the long summer vacation students have every year. If kids are not filling this time with beneficial things that will help them grow and advance,

---

[11] Al-Wasiti, *'Uyoon Al-Hukm wal-Mawa'ez*, 471.
[12] Al-Majlisi, *Bihar Al-Anwar*, 74:419.

there is no doubt they will fall into free-time. That free-time will turn into useless activities that will likely bring them no benefit or may even harm them.

In God's perspective, mankind is His greatest creation. Thus, his creation did not come in vain. Mankind was created for a high and noble purpose. It only makes sense that our lives follow suit with our God-given purpose. Therefore, we should utilize every moment we have to work towards that goal and strive towards our destiny and our reason for creation. Free-time and the lack of filling our time are a hindrance and waste of our energy – making our being vain, which is opposed to our God-given purpose. Our narrations emphasize God's heavy disapproval with people who waste their time. An example of this is the saying of Imam Al-Kadhim (a): *"God dislikes the servant who sleeps all the time, and the servant that wastes his time."*[13]

Mankind was not created for sleep; sleep has its role just like food and drink – they are used by a person to maintain a healthy life. This does not mean a person is to turn his life into sleep and laziness because we were not created for that. Likewise, we were not created to be bored and waste our time either. That free-time and wastefulness drag a person into pastime, perversion, and becoming farther from the essential goal for mankind's creation. And thus, we notice this relevant passage in the supplication of Imam Zain Al-Abideen (a), '*Makarim Al-Akhlaq*':

> O God, bless Muhammad and his Household. Spare me the concerns that distract me. Employ me in the matters

---

13 Al-Saduq, *Men La Yahduruhu Al-Faqih*, 3:169.

*that You will ask me about tomorrow. And let me pass my
days in that for which You have created me...* [14]

HOW TO FILL YOUR TIME

We discussed the importance of filling one's time and not
letting it pass in vain. Now let us turn to how we should
actually go about filling our time in a beneficial way.

First, it is essential to categorize our time and prioritize our
tasks and activities for their suitable times in the day. We
need to prioritize based on importance and time sensitivity,
because life does not allow us to accomplish every single
little thing we may list. It would be extremely useful to put
together a daily schedule of the things we need to accomplish. This should be applied to work, making a living, family matters, worship, enriching one's cultural experience and
knowledge base, etc. Therefore, by scheduling one's days
and prioritizing tasks a person can truly take advantage of
his time instead of wasting away the precious hours of his
life.

Second, it is also important to avoid busying ourselves with
games and entertainment with the excuse that we need to be
entertained in order to fill our time and let time pass. Of
course, there are types of entertainment that are fine for us
to have – as long as they are within the boundaries of religious law. As human beings we need downtime with some
fun and entertainment in order to get through the difficulties of life. It helps us push through our hardships and encourages us to move forward. However, to be always busy

---

[14] Imam Zain Al-Abideen (a), *Al-Saheefa Al-Sajjadiyya*, Dua Makarim Al-Akhlaq.

with games and entertainment is not becoming of us. Humanity is greater and more purposed than to waste life away on entertainment and games. The Commander of the Faithful (a) said, *"Know that this world is the place of trial. Whoever here wastes any hour of his time will regret it on the Day of Judgment."*[15]

Third, we must understand that the best things to fill our free time are the things that please God and bring us closer to Him. An example of this is worship, whereby we feel the sweetness of not being busy with other things. This kind of beneficial free time, in turn, is desirable. Imam Ali Zein Al-Abideen (a) said in one of his supplications, *"Let me taste, through some of Your boundless bounties, the flavor of having free time to do what You love, and striving in what brings me closer to You..."*[16] Another example is seeking knowledge that will benefit us bring us light and closeness to God. Beyond worship and seeking knowledge, it can be anything with a worldly benefit and a connected benefit to the afterlife.

Fourth, it is vital for parents to be concerned with filling their kids' free-time wisely. Parents should not leave their children to tend to that problem on their own, because it could be the cause of their children straying away from God and getting into trouble or simply being vain. This is a responsibility that parents have towards their kids. Raising children mandates following up with your kids to fill their time and make sure that they are benefiting from the activities they are doing, instead of wasting their life away.

---

[15] Al-Radi, *Nahj Al-Balagha*, 3:116, Letter 59.
[16] Imam Zein Al-Abideen (a), *Al-Saheefa Al-Sajjadiya*, Supplication 146: His Supplication on the Day of Arafa.

Finally, there should be a focused effort by the believers for studying and providing solutions to the problem of free-time that affects so many youth. Programs and projects that bring awareness to these problems should be initiated. The problem must be addressed by all of us collectively, to encourage a lifestyle that fills the time of our sons and daughters with matters that will help them grow, nurture their minds, and benefit them, their community, and their nation.

THE PROPHET (S)

In the name of God, the most Beneficent, the most Merciful

There is certainly a good exemplar for you in the Apostle of God—for those who look forward to God and the Last Day, and remember God much. [1]

THE ROLE MODEL

The day of the passing of the Grand Prophet Muhammad (s) was a great tragedy for the human race, as mankind lost the greatest individual to ever walk the Earth – rather, lost the greatest creation of God. His noble spirit and sacred essence that God has favored over all creation with no exception and given it the highest of status departed this world on the twenty-eighth of the month of Safar. What great tragedy did that day bear? With his death, the time of divine inspiration and revelation ended. The Commander of the Faithful would eulogize him saying

> *May my father and my mother be your ransom [O Messenger of God!] Your death marked the end of what had not*

---

[1] The Holy Quran. Chapter 33 [The Parties; Arabic: *Al-Ahzab*]. Verse 21.

ended with the death of other prophets; the end of prophet-
hood, prophecy, and heavenly messages. Your [tragedy] is so
unique [in its gravity] that [remembering] it has become a
source of consolation for [tragedies concerning] all others;
and your [tragedy] is so encompassing that all are inflicted
by it equally. If you had not ordered endurance and forbade
impatience, we would have run out of our store of tears. Our
ailment would have not subsided and this grief would not
have ended. And that would have been too little [relative to
the tragedy of your loss]. But this [death or sadness] is a
matter that cannot be reversed nor is it possible to push it
away. May my father and my mother be your ransom; do
remember us before your Lord and take care of us.

His tragedy is far greater than any other tragedy. The calamity that befell this nation with his death cannot be compared
to any other calamity. Who else can be described as "a mercy to the worlds?" Not only a mercy to his followers, but to
all mankind. Not only a mercy to mankind, but to all creation. God says in His Holy Book "*We did not send you but as a*
mercy to all the nations."[2] The scope of this mercy is boundless,
reaching even the greatest of angels:

It is narrated that the Prophet (s) asked Gabriel at the time
of revelation of this verse 'have you benefited at all from this
mercy?' [Gabriel] answered 'yes. I was fearful of the Day of
Judgment, but I felt safety in your presence when God re-
vealed to you the following verse in my praise: 'powerful
and eminent with the Lord of the Throne.*[34]

---

[2] The Holy Quran. Chapter 21 [The Prophets; Arabic: *Al-Anbiaa*]. Verse 107.
[3] The Holy Quran. Chapter 81 [The Winding; Arabic: *Al-Takweer*]. Verse 20.
[4] Al-Majlisi, *Bihar Al-Anwar*, 16:306.

It is also narrated that the Prophet (s) said "*I am a mercy gifted [to all creation].*"[5]

Therefore, the Prophet (s) is a mercy of God that has been sent to save mankind. The Prophet (s) was the one tasked with bringing faith to all mankind, so they are all within the scope of this mercy. However, the believer will benefit from this mercy whereas the non-believer may not. The Prophet (s) is like a doctor who has offered to treat anyone who would be willing to receive the treatment. He is a mercy to all. Whoever comes to him to receive his treatment has benefited from this mercy. Whoever refuses to receive his treatment has deprived himself of that mercy. His actions do not limit the scope of the mercy; the mercy remains encompassing of all.

BENEFITING FROM HIS EXAMPLE

We must strive to benefit from this divine mercy in all its aspects. The happiness of mankind and salvation from the pits of darkness that we may fall into can only be attained through the mercy that is the Grand Prophet (s). We must abide by his teachings and guidance. We must study the details of his life; his actions, his words, and his ratification of others' actions. All these are manifestations of God's commands. The most important means by which we can benefit from the blessings of this divine personality is through taking him as an example and a role model. This is a Quranic concept that God has stressed upon in His words; "*There is certainly a good exemplar for you in the Apostle of God—for those*

---

[5] Ibid. 16:115.

who look forward to God and the Last Day, and remember God much."[6]

THE PROPHET'S (S) ACTIONS

The traditions of the Prophet (s) consist of much more than his words, they also include his actions and his ratification of others' actions. His (s) traditions are the main source of Islamic teachings after the Holy Quran. Generally, every one of his actions is thus as much a tradition that must be followed as his words. The Prophet's (s) commands are given verbally at times; he may command an individual to undertake a certain action. But at times, his commands may come in the form of actions that are indistinguishable in their indication from verbal commands. For that reason, the study of the Prophet's (s) actions is of utmost importance for any scholar of Islam.

In addition, the actions of the Prophet (s) do not differ or lag behind God's wishes. The All-Wise God sends prophets to be role models and to be trusted as deliverers of the Divine message. This requires exemplary character, in words and action, in line with God's will. God chose certain individuals whom He knew would do this freely, out of devotion to God. The Prophet's (s) words are not spoken of fallible whim, but rather are words inspired and emanating from God, the Lord of Honor and Majesty. *"Nor does he speak out of desire: it is just a revelation that is revealed [to him]"*[7] And because his actions are as important as his speech, the Prophet's (s) actions must be identical to God's wishes and

---

[6] The Holy Quran. Chapter 33 [The Parties; Arabic: *Al-Ahzab*]. Verse 21.
[7] The Holy Quran. Chapter 53 [The Star; Arabic: *Al-Najm*]. Verses 3, 4.

in harmony with His will. Otherwise, people may reasonably lose confidence in the Prophet's integrity and the goal of sending the Prophet as an exemplary role model would not be accomplished, Abiding by his verbal commands has its effects on a person's closeness to God. Modeling our behavior after his example has the same effect. Moreover, we find that the Immaculate Imams (a) warn against separating between the two. As the narration of Imam Sajjad (a) says, *"indeed, the people that are most detested by God are those that follow a leader's words but do not follow his actions."*[8] Chanting slogans is not nearly as important as living up to them. We must make sure that our actions conform to the teachings of the Prophet (a). Whoever takes the Prophet (s) as a role model must strive to observe both his words and his actions.

The Immaculate Prophet (s) – who is a perfect leader and guide towards God, and the individual who knows God best – knows best the methods for attaining closeness to God. Therefore, his actions are the perfect example of what drives an individual closer to God. We cannot imagine that the Prophet (s) would take any action that would take him away from God, or that he would possess any characteristic that would distance him from God. He is the most perfect individual. He is the best of creation. So taking the Prophet (s) as a role model could only lead to closeness to God. Rather, it is the best method and the shortest path to reaching that closeness. And that closeness is the greatest goal for a human and the means to true happiness, away from the darkness that surrounds human life.

---

[8] Al-Kulayni, *Al-Kafi*, 8:234.

It is also interesting to note that the command in the holy verse was absolute and unrestricted. This means that we must not only take the Prophet (s) as our role model when it comes to the greater things in life, but also in every simple step along the way. So we see that the Commander of the Faithful instructs us to follow the model of the Prophet (s) in the greatest of issues:

> *Patience is an obligation upon the [special group] vested with authority because of God's statement to His Prophet (s)* 'So be patient just as the resolute among the apostles were patient.' *God has also made this an obligation upon His friends and those obedient to Him when He said* 'There is certainly a good exemplar for you in the Apostle of God—for those who look forward to God and the Last Day, and remember God much.'[910]

We are also instructed to follow the Prophet's (s) example in the simplest of things. Imam Sadiq (a) says, "*When the Prophet (s) would pray the evening prayer, he would ask for water for his ablution and his Siwaak[11] to be put covered near his head [as he rested]...*"[12] The Imam (a) would continue to describe how the Prophet (s) would pray Salat Al-Layl. Then the Imam (a) recited the holy verse, "*There is certainly a good exemplar for you in the Apostle....*"[13] This may seem as a simple thing if taken at face value, yet the Imam (a) still instructs us to follow the

---

[9] The Holy Quran. Chapter 33 [The Parties; Arabic: *Al-Ahzab*]. Verse 21.

[10] Al-Tabrasi, *Al-Ihtijaj*, 1:356.

[11] *Siwaak* or *Miswaak* is an oral hygiene instrument made from the twigs of a certain species of tree commonly found in the Middle East.

[12] Al-Amili, *Wasa'el Al-Shia*, 1:356.

[13] The Holy Quran. Chapter 33 [The Parties; Arabic: *Al-Ahzab*]. Verse 21.

Prophet's (s) example in this regard. There may be wisdom with value beyond measure even in the seemingly simplest of acts.

WE CAN ALL FOLLOW HIS EXAMPLE

Three conditions must be fulfilled before an individual truly models their behavior after the Prophet's (s).

First, the intention of seeking closeness to God should be the primary reason for following the teachings and the example of the Prophet (s). A person who does not seek God's mercy will not have the necessary motivation to take the Prophet (s) as a role model. Without the intention of seeking the pleasure of God and closeness to Him, we cannot imagine that anyone would be following in the footsteps of the Prophet (s).

Second, the individual must believe in the hereafter, or else will not be able to take the Prophet (s) as a role model. If a person does not believe in a Day of Judgment, he/she will not even think to model his behavior after the Prophet (s), as he will not see any need for it. For indeed, in every step, the Prophet (s) showed the path of excellence for the Hereafter as well as for this world. Even what seem to be matters of this world, such as business transactions, can have a special spiritual dimension in the Prophetic tradition.

Third, the individual must be in constant remembrance of God. Remembrance plays a great role. If a person has not built his heart with the remembrance of God, he/she will not be able to walk in the Prophet's (s) footsteps. We must drive away Satan and light our paths with remembrance so that we can truly follow the Prophet's (s) example. As Abu Thar said, "*I entered the mosque one day while the Prophet (s) was in it… He said to me: 'Read the Book of God and remember Him profusely. It will be a remembrance for you in the heavens and a light for you on Earth.*'[14] Imam Ali (a) also said, "*the remembrance of God enlightens the insight and comforts the conscience.*"[15]

An individual who wishes to follow the example of the Prophet (s) needs a source that shows him the Prophet's (s) example. He needs something that keeps Satan away so that he does not slip. Both of these can be achieved through remembrance of God.

So to follow the Prophet's (s) example, you need three things: the intention of seeking closeness to God, and the belief in the hereafter that drives an individual to follow the Prophet's example; and the remembrance of God as the fuel that allows the individual to push forward on this path.

LESSONS FROM HIS LIFE

We are in utmost need, especially in these dire circumstances that humanity is passing through, to mention the qualities of the Prophet of Islam (s). Without the right prescription for physical, spiritual and intellectual well-being, humanity is heading towards the edge of a cliff. The true teachings of Islam and the example of the Grand Prophet of Islam, Prophet Muhammad (s), are the recipe for success on all levels. We will point out a few of the illustrious examples of his life here.

---

14 Al-Saduq, *Al-Khisal*, 525.
15 Al-Wasiti, *'Uyoon Al-Hikam wa Al-Mawa'ez*, 255.

His Worship

It is impossible for us to imagine a creation that is more subservient to God than the Prophet (s). The virtue, honor, and status of a human go back to their worship and their knowledge of God. The Prophet (s) is be best of creation because he is the most subservient to God. It is enough to point out that all Muslims bear witness in their prayers that Muhammad is the servant of God, even before recognizing him as the Messenger of God.[16] Even Imam Ali ibn Al-Hussein, who was known as "the Best of Worshippers" attested to the Prophet's (s) status in worship. He (a) was once asked about his own worship as compared to the worship of his grandfather the Commander of the Faithful. The Imam (a) replied, *"my worship as compared to the worship of my grandfather is much like the worship of my grandfather if compared to the worship of the Messenger of God (s)."*[17]

An even clearer indication of this can be seen in God's conversation with the Prophet (s) about the Prophet's (s) worship. God says, *"Ta Ha! We did not send down to you the Quran that you should be miserable, but only as an admonition to him who fears [his Lord]."*[18] It is reported that Imam Al-Kadhim (a) narrated the following on behalf of his forefathers,

> *The Commander of the Faithful said: Indeed, the Messenger of God (s) stood [in prayer] for ten years on the tips of his toes, until his feet were swollen and his face became yellow. He would spend the entire night [in prayer]... until*

---

[16] In the *Tashahhud* part near the end of prayer, Muslims read some variation of the following: "I bear witness that there is no God but God and that Muhammad is His Servant and His Messenger."

[17] Al-Majlisi, *Bihar Al-Anwar*, 41:149.

[18] The Holy Quran. Chapter 20 [Arabic: *Ta Ha*]. Verses 1-3.

God told him 'Ta Ha! We did not send down to you
the Quran that you should be miserable.*[19,20]*

Oh, how we need to turn to God with our worship so that
he can light our path and rescue us from our present state.
If the Prophet (s), who is the best of all creation without a
doubt, performs such astonishing acts of worship, then it is
imperative for us to follow his example. Let us take him as a
role model so that our relationship to him can play its role
in driving us closer to God.

His Patience

The Prophet (s) had great patience that was astonishing at
all levels. He was patient in his worship. He was patient with
tragedy. He was patient in his delivery of the message of
God. He bore what no other man had to bear. He (s) said,
and he is surely the most truthful, *"no prophet was harmed to
the same extent that I was harmed."*[21] His patience with his people was truly astonishing. With all the harm that they did to
him, all their mockery of him, and their stance against his
message of truth, we see him turn towards God and pray
"Oh God, forgive my people, for they do not know."[22] Moreover, he
would live with all those who would harm him, knowing of
all the harm that they would cause him and his family. He
knew all this, but it did not have any effect on the way he
dealt with them, and they did not feel any change in the
Prophet's (s) relationship with them.

---

[19] The Holy Quran. Chapter 20 [Arabic: *Ta Ha*]. Verses 1, 2.

[20] Al-Huwayzi, *Noor Al-Thaqalayn*, 3:367.

[21] Al-Majlisi, *Bihar Al-Anwar*, 39:56.

[22] Ibn Tawuus, *Iqbal Al-A'mal*, 1:385.

We see the most astonishing feats of patience accomplished in the most difficult of situations. It is enough to cite the testimony of Imam Ali (a) when he says, *"In the most vigorous moments of battle we would seek the protection of the Messenger of God (s). No one would be closer to the enemies than him."*[23]

We have the utmost need to draw inspiration from the patience of the Prophet (s) in these difficult times.

His Mercy

What can we say about the mercy of the Prophet (s) when God the Exalted addresses the Prophet (s) with the following: *"We did not send you but as a mercy to all the nations."*[24] What testimony can be greater than this? What can we add to the great description that God gave to His Prophet (s)? It is enough to mention the great pain that he would go through for the sake of the nonbelievers. Mercy would encompass him as he would call to God. They would reply with violent force. God would comfort his Prophet (s) with the following words: *"These are the signs of the Manifest Book. [Will you] imperil your life [out of distress for their sake] when they refuse to believe?"*[25] When God sees the great deal of suffering that the Prophet (s) went through to spread the message and how he was hurt when they did not answer his call, He would tell him not to worry about their disbelief and He would comfort him with the following:

> *Is someone the evil of whose conduct is presented as decorous to him, so he regards it as good, [like one who is truly virtu-*

---

[23] Al-Radi, *Nahj Al-Balagha*, 4:61.
[24] The Holy Quran. Chapter 21 [The Prophets; Arabic: *Al-Anbia*]. Verse 107.
[25] The Holy Quran. Chapter 26 [The Poets; Arabic: *Al-Shu'ara*]. Verses 2, 3.

ous?] Indeed God leads astray whomever He wishes, and guides whomever He wishes. So do not fret yourself to death regretting for them. Indeed God knows best what they do.[26]

This is a clear call to the Prophet (s) not to let himself go in grief for the unbelievers.

These examples of the Prophet's (s) great character should suffice for now. We must seek to follow his example in these issues and take him as our role model. We are in critical need for merciful hearts that would encompass anyone that may be different or disagree with us. We are in need for patience in calling for the truth and for the path of God. The driving force that pushes one along on this sacred path is the force of worship and utmost dedication to God Almighty.

We end with a few words of the Commander of the Faithful (a) encouraging us to follow the example of the Prophet (s):

> *Therefore, one should follow His Prophet, tread in his footsteps and enter through his gate. Otherwise he will not be safe from ruin. Certainly, God made Muhammad (s) a sign for the Day of Judgment, a conveyor of tidings for Paradise, and a warner of retribution.*
>
> *He left this world [indifferent towards bounties] but entered upon the next world in safety. He did not lay one stone upon another (to make a house) till he departed and responded to the call of God. How great is God's blessing in that He blessed us with the Prophet as a predecessor whom we follow and a leader behind whom we tread.*

---

[26] The Holy Quran. Chapter 35 [The Originator; Arabic: *Faatir*]. Verse 8.

IMAM HUSSAIN'S (A)
RENAISSANCE

In the name of God, the most Beneficent, the most Merciful

Imam Hussain (a) wrote to his brother Muhammad ibn Ali stating,

> *In the Name of God the Beneficent the Merciful... From Hussain son of Ali to Muhammad son of Ali and those near him from the children of Hashem... whoever follows me will be a martyr and whoever does not will not realize victory.*[1]

Ashura, this eternal holy saga, remains a university throughout the centuries. The seekers of truth take from it lessons and morals that they need in their time and place. This saga has boggled the minds of writers and researchers, indeed it has intrigued all people as to why this university is so special. Possibly one of the most beautiful answers to this intrigue comes from the words of one of our high scholars about Imam Hussain and his cause:

---

[1] Ibn Qawlawiya, *Kamil Al-Ziyarat*, 157.

*The cause of Hussain (a) is the same cause of the Holy
Quran. This cause is not limited to the time when it was
sent, but rather renews in every age and treats and cures the
problems of each era. He is alive and provides rejuvenation
like the sun and the moon. Just like it has been narrated by
the Ahlulbayt (a), Hussain (a) is himself the speaking
Quran. We must understand his cause and movement so
that we are able to accept its revelation and inspiration in
every era.[2]*

Writers, researchers, lecturers, and intellectuals still, to this
day, speak of Imam Hussain (a) and his renaissance. They
continue to discover lessons and morals from his movement, and thus his remembrance continues to be renewed.
We can understand how Imam Hussain (a) was victorious
through his martyrdom because he was able to defeat his
enemies and wipe them out from the remembrance of history. He continued to sit on the throne above all conquerors
through the establishment of his moral values and the accomplishment of his goals.

God has given Hussain (a) a special place in the souls of the
believers whereby the soul does not tire from his remembrance no matter how frequent. Rather, the lamentation only increases whenever we remember him and attend the
gatherings of his commemoration. The renaissance of
Hussain (a) brought forth rich intellectual thought in several
dimensions. The reason for this renewal in commemoration
is that the individual who knows and seeks God will,
through this renaissance, find the clearest paths of guidance
and connection to God. Politicians and policy makers will

---

[2] Al-Hakeem, *Thawrat Al-Hussain (a)*, 60.

find the pinnacle of political tactics, strategy, and maturity. Brave men and women will see in this eternal saga the greatest heroism and bravery witnessed by history. Leaders will witness the keenest show of leadership evidenced by the greatest sacrifice made by any human being. In his every move, Imam Hussain (a) was reviving the cause of his ultimate role model, Prophet Muhammad (s), within an unprecedented set of challenging variables. In every field, we find that the rise of Imam Hussain (a) formed a fundamental ground of teaching and instruction for that particular field. But there is one particular dimension that demands special attention because it is a focal point of Prophet Muhammad's (s) message. Hence, we must turn to it and try to understand it further. I am referring to the ethical dimension in Imam Hussain's (a) movement. Let us discuss it in the following points.

ETHICS IN IMAM HUSSAIN'S (A) MOVEMENT

This dimension was a working essential element in Imam Hussain's (a) movement because the primary goal of the movement was to shock and reawaken the moral conscience of the community. Probably one of the root causes of the absence or death of one's conscience is a defect in the ethics of the community. A community that is built on ethics and lives in accordance with ethics is a community that is alive in its conscience, and thus cannot be defeated. A community that has left its ethics, however, is a dead community no matter how large it becomes and how great its resources.

This ethical dimension is in fact one of the most important elements of all prophetic missions. The Holy Prophet (s) considered teaching ethics as a focal point of his mission, *"Indeed, I have been sent to perfect the best of ethics."*[3]

The most effective way to conquer and control a community is by killing its moral conscience. And that does not happen except by ridding the community of its principles, values and ethics. For a community that lives by the principles of honesty, loyalty, sacrifice, courage and generosity is one that cannot be dominated, controlled or conquered. You cannot play or toy with such a community. But when such a community loses these principles and values, it is moral conscience dies along with any motivation to live a noble life. And in that case, such a community will accept anything in order to ensure its interests, desires and wants.

The focus of the Umayyads was to destroy the morals and ethics of the Islamic community. This is evidenced by Yazid's first speech upon becoming Caliph after his father Muawiya, luring people in through time off, money, relaxation and luxury:

> ...*Muawiya used to take you on expeditions through the seas... and I will not be taking you on such expeditions... and keep you in the lands of the Romans during the winter, and I will not keep any of you in such lands in such harsh times... and he would give you your payments in thirds, but I will give that to you in whole lump sums.*[4]

---

[3] Al-Majlisi, *Bihar Al-Anwar*, 16:210.

[4] Al-Hakeem, *Thawrat Al-Hussain (a)*, 141. Citing: Ibn Katheer, *Al-Bidaya wal-Nihaya*, 8:153.

And even clearer than this example are the words of Ibn Ziyad, Yazid's governor in Kufa, as he packaged the arguments to people to go out and fight Imam Hussain (a):

> *You found the Umayyads as your hearts please. And this is Yazid, you know him as one with a good, solid, praiseworthy path... he honors people and makes them rich with wealth... he increased your sustenance hundreds-fold... he is now ordering me to give you all these riches and take you out to wage war on his enemy Hussain... so listen to him and obey this command.[5]*

Imam Hussain (a) would describe this painful reality that turned the Muslims from people who sought God and fought for His cause to people who are bought and sold with money. This was due to the fact that they lost their moral conscience, their will and and sold their afterlife for their limited pleasures in this world. The Imam (a) would tell his companions:

> *People are slaves to this world and religion is only words on their tongues. They hold on to it so long as their means of living are secured. But if they are tested with tribulation the true believers will be less... You see what has come upon us. This world has changed and become corrupted. What was commonly known as right has withered away. Nothing is left but a trace like the last few droplets of an empty cup and a lowly life like a tainted unwholesome pasture. Do you not see that truth [and righteousness] are not being acted upon [and abided by]? And that falsehood is not being discouraged? So let the believer long for meeting God. For I do*

---

[5] Ibid. Citing: Al-Muqarram, *Maqtal Al-Hussain (a)*, 198-199.

not see death [for God's sake] except as happiness, and life
with these oppressors except as weariness.[6]

From the aforementioned passages, the Imam (a) places his thumb on the wound. The corruption of ethics and the lack of moral values are the reasons that many Muslims stopped caring about religion and focused their attention only on matters of this world.

The Holy Quran and the noble narrations point to the importance of the ethical dimension of the life of the community, its advancement, and its happiness. The verses and narrations discuss the extent of harm that is brought to mankind by losing ethics. It moves people away from the grounds of nobility that God established for us. Furthermore, that loss changes individuals from servants of God to servants of this finite world, which will experience an end to its pleasures through its mere death.

In the movement of Imam Hussain (a), and his blessed renaissance, there was a focus on establishing a number of ethical principles. The goal was to broadcast these principles through the movement of Imam Hussain (a) and the effect it would have on the people in all of its dimensions. Similarly, these ethical principles were established in such a manner that they can be pointed to by humanity, across all the generations, and benefit from the light that is the movement of Hussain (a).

---

[6] Al-Muqarram, *Maqtal Al-Hussain (a)*, Pg. 192-193. Citing: *Al-Tabari, Tareekh Al-Tabari*, 4:305; Al-Andalusi, *Al-'Uqd Al-Fareed*, 2:312; and Al-Asbahani, *Hulliyat Al-Awliya'*, 2:39.

Practical Examples in His Movement

It is not possible to confine all of the ethical principles that Imam Hussain (a) practiced and established through his blessed renaissance. However, we can point to some of the most important principles that no community should neglect. By holding on to the following principles and values, our communities can advance, move forward, and work along the godly path that God wished for humanity.

Honesty and Transparency

Honesty in our dealing with one another is among the most significant ethical principles that Imam Hussain (a) established. From the beginning of his movement, the Imam (a) did not give people false hope in spoils of war, well-being, or victory. Instead, he went against the norm of most political leaders who only cared for rallying the masses without regard to the reality facing the people, their conscience, and their intentions. Imam Hussain (a) was clear from the very beginning in the first announcement of his movement before leaving Mecca:

> *Praise be to God, everything is by His will, there is no strength save in God, and praise be upon His Messenger. Death is to the son of Adam like a necklace is to the neck of a young lady. O' how I long for my forefathers, like the longing of Jacob to Joseph. And I will meet the best of ends. Whoever would sacrifice his heart for us and is determined to meet God, let him journey with us for I am departing tomorrow morning God willing.[7]*

---

[7] Ibid. 166.

Imam Hussain (a) did not trick anyone or force anyone to go on his journey with him. He did not use the methods of the Umayyads in forcing people to fight or buying people's loyalty to militarize them and have them become soldiers. Honesty and transparency are the features that distinguished Imam Hussain (a) and his companions from the rest of people. Initially, there was a huge group of people that followed Imam Hussain (a) thinking that he was going to take over the governance, as much of the matters were established for him completely. But then came the news of Muslim Ibn Aqeel, the ambassador of Imam Hussain (a) to Kufa. The people of Kufa had betrayed him, had him executed and ultimately broke their promise to support the movement of the Imam (a). Imam Hussain (a) did not keep this news from the people; rather, he shared it with them. He gave them the choice to stay or leave. Those initial large numbers dwindled down to a small group of loyal companions.

Imam Hussain (a) could have launched an all out marketing campaign to gain recruits by promising them riches and wealth. But that was not his character – he was honest with his men. As the heir of the Holy Prophet (s), there was no doubt he would establish these ethical principles and deal with reality instead of fraud and deception. This was the difference between Ahlulbayt (a) and the military that stood against them. Probably one of the hardest stands that Imam Hussain (a) had to make was on the night of the tenth of Muharram. He gathered his companions and family members and said:

I do not know of any companions better than my companions, nor a family more pure and rooted than my own. May God reward you on my behalf. I see that the day they will transgress against us is tomorrow. I give you leave to take off in the night, there is no blame or fault on you if you leave. The night has shrouded you, so ride into the night. Let each one of you take a member of my household [as a guardian] and disperse in the lands and cities. May God reward you all. These people ask for me, not for you... and if they get to me they will be too preoccupied to go after anyone else.[8]

So the Imam (a) gave his companions and family members permission to leave him and did not force them to stay with him; rather, he relieved them of their duties towards him. But even with that, we find that this small honorable group refused to leave the Imam (a) and was determined to live and die beside him. Through this honorable stand, Imam Hussain (a) proved to us the necessity of leaders to live with their populace in a state of honesty and transparency. The leaders must not take advantage of their followers and supporters without their knowledge of the reality. Likewise, leaders must not take their followers for granted. This is extremely important in the validity of the movement and its advancement.

Sacrifice

Islam has given great focus to sacrifice and considers it among the noblest of ethical principles. It is enough that we see the Holy Quran point to this ethical virtue when God

---

[8] Ibid. 513.

commends the Ansar for their stance with the Muhajireen and the sacrifices they made. God said:

> [They are as well] for those who were settled in the land and [abided] in faith before them, who love those who migrate toward them, and do not find in their breasts any privation for that which is given to them, but prefer [the Immigrants] to themselves, though poverty be their own lot. And those who are saved from their own greed—it is they who are the felicitous.[9]

The history of Islam is filled, from its very beginning, with wondrous stories that show that this particularity was present in the midst of the Muslims. Many of them espoused this honorable moral trait. However, the weakening of ethical principles came as a result of abandoning the teachings of Prophet Muhammad (s) and turning away from the righteous guardians of the faith – Ahlulbayt (a). The many conquests that were undertaken and the indulgement in wealth and worldly pleasures could not cover up the moral decay that had set in. Ethics were further weakened by the Umayyads' role in dissolving and ultimately eliminating the Muslims' adherence and identification with moral virtues. This specific trait was weakened just like other ethical virtues were weakened.

The school of Ashura came to reestablish this virtue, whereby Ahlulbayt (a) struggled in this pursuit with Imam Hussain (a) and his companions at the forefront of this struggle. They sacrificed themselves for the sake of raising the word of God. As one poet says in Arabic, "Giving one-

---

[9] The Holy Quran. Chapter 59 [The Reckoning; Arabic: *Al-Hashr*]. Verse 9.

self [as a sacrifice] is the epitome of generosity." This is in addition to some of the phenomena that human beings cannot fully comprehend and that can only be produced by that holy household – Ahlulbayt (a). That household was the one that sacrificed for three consecutive days, as it fed the poor, the orphan, and the prisoner and remained hungry. This is the household that birthed the likes of Al-Abbas (a), this hero who sacrificed for his brother and master Imam Hussain (a). He would head to the banks of the Euphrates river only to fill a satchel of water to quench the thirst of the women and children who had been without water for three days. Finally arriving, he kneeled down to take a sip of water. With all of his thirst and dehydration, he remembered the thirst of Imam Hussain (a) and the rest of the family. As he let the water go, it is reported that he said to himself:

O self, compared to Hussain you are nothing... and after him may you not live another day... this is Hussain coming close to his death... and you wish to drink the cold pure water? By God this is not an act of my faith.

Abbas did not drink in consolation of his brother Al-Hussain (a) and his family. Who could compare to the sacrifice and consolation of Al-Abbas (a) whereby he would prevent himself from drinking because his brother did not drink? He put his brother before himself and proceeded to return to the camp to get him water. Unfortunately he did not reach Hussain (a) or his family because he was killed by the treachery of Yazid's soldiers. This is one of many illustrations of sacrifice in the movement of Imam Hussian (a) and his companions.

Chivalry

Of the most noble and honorable virtues of Imam Hussain (a) was chivalry. He illustrated the highest forms of chivalry in his blessed revolution, which can be summarized in the following:

Imam Hussain (a) gave water to his enemies and their horses. The battalion of Al-Hur Al-Riyahi was ordered to stop the Imam (a) in Karbala before reaching Kufa. This battalion, loyal to Yazid, reached Imam Hussain (a) in such a dire state of thirst and dehydration. And they had come to stop the Imam (a). Nonetheless, when Imam Hussain (a) witnessed the thirst of his enemies, he ordered his companies to give water to the soldiers along with their horses. Who could compare to this show of chivalry? A man sees his enemies in such a weak state, knowing their plans against him, and with that he chooses to quench their thirst.

Al-Hur Al-Riyahi was responsible for much of the suffering that Imam Hussain (a), his companions, and family initially endured in Karbala. Regardless, the Imam (a) welcomed Al-Hur's repentance to God when he came forward on the Day of Ashura asking for forgiveness. On that day, Al-Hur looked at the two camps and saw Heaven and Hell. Pacing back and forth, pale in the face, he made up his mind and made his way to the camp of Imam Hussain (a) – he chose Heaven. Coming down from his horse, with his head bowed in shame, he called out: "O' God to you I turn, so accept my repentance. I have frightened the hearts of your loved ones and the children of your Prophet. O' Aba Abdillah, I am repenting… is there repentance for me?" Imam Hussain (a) replied, *"Yes. God will accept your repentance."*[10]

This was the heart of Hussain (a). This was the heart so dear to the Messenger of God (s). A heart full of mercy, even to those who stopped him in Karbala. How could Hussain (a) be any other way, when God made him the spiritual heir to the one sent as a Mercy to all Mankind?

Imam Hussain (a) was adamant on not starting the battle. He did not permit any of his companions to launch any arrows or spears at the enemy until the enemy launched first. Omar ibn Saad released the first arrow saying, "Witness for me before the Prince (Yazid) that I was the first to cast his arrow!" At that point, Imam Hussain (a) permitted his companions to respond. This was a true stance of chivalry and honor. Imam Hussain (a) could have easily taken preemptive measures and killed a number of Omar ibn Saad's soldiers; however, he refused to do anything of the like. His objective was to establish value and virtue and he made a point not to be the one who started the fight. Value and Virtue were victorious on that day.

The Imam (a) continues to establish and consolidate these moral values like loyalty, sacrifice, bravery, and nobility, amongst others. He is able to do so due to the eternal nature of his movement and renaissance. As long as he is remembered, these virtues and values will also be remembered. The memory of Hussain (a) will remain as long as this world exists. This is one thing that makes the words of Imam Hussain (a) so true: *"Whoever does not follow me will not*

---

[10] Al-Muqarram, *Maqtal Al-Hussain (a)*, 182.

realize victory..." What victory is greater than being eternal in memory and principle? Thus, these ethical virtues and godly principles will remain forever in his remembrance. Let every human being live in the love of Hussain (a) as he longs to follow his example of values and ethics.

THE DEATH OF
CONSCIENCE

In the name of God, the most Beneficent, the most Merciful

Then your hearts hardened after that; so they are like stones, or even harder. For there are some stones from which streams gush forth, and there are some of them that split, and water issues from them, and there are some that fall for the fear of God. And God is not oblivious of what you do.[1]

As we stand before the details of the tragic memory of Ashura, we find ourselves before a battle that has escaped the measures of any other battle. One of the distinct characteristics of this battle was the brutality that was used against Imam Hussain (a), his companions, and his holy family. History does not speak of a greater tragedy, nor do we hear of any actions that have shamed humanity like the crimes that were carried out against the family of the Holy Prophet (s) and their companions. There are numerous illustrations of these crimes written by historians. It is possible to point in a general sense to some of the illustrations of the horrid

---

[1] The Holy Quran. Chapter 2 [The Cow; Arabic: *Al-Baqara*]. Verse 74.

crimes executed by the enemies of God against His Messenger and humanity. They became a notorious gang that are damned by God, his angels, history, and everyone who has an atom's worth of humanity in their hearts. They disgraced humanity through their crimes that will forever be etched in history. Some of the many disgraceful crimes that took place are briefly illustrated in the following.

Imam Hussain (a), his companions, and family members were all banned from drinking water. The women and children suffered from dehydration for over three days. They had committed no crime for which to be punished. This painful image is crowned with Imam Hussain (a) going out into the battlefield with his newborn child. He holds his child up high for the entire camp of the enemy to see. He tells them, "*If the adults have a sin [to answer for], then what is the sin of the children?*" They refused to give him water. So, he told them to take the newborn baby and give him water themselves. To that request, the army fell into a dispute. Some of the soldiers expressed some compassion and said that they should give water to the baby. The others, however, remained cold and screamed out rejecting the request of the Imam (a). Omar ibn Saad ordered Harmala ibn Kahil Al-Asady, "End the dispute of our soldiers." As one of the best archers in the army's ranks, Harmala understood the message. He took an arrow and aimed it, not at Hussain (a) but at the newborn child. With that arrow he slaughtered the youngest son of the Imam (a). As the child's blood flowed from his neck, Imam Hussain (a) caught the rivers of red in the palm of his hand and cast the blood into the sky. *"Not one drop ever fell,"* said Imam Al-Baqir (a).[2]

What pains the heart even further is the illustration of how Imam Hussain (a) himself was killed. It is difficult to put pen to paper and remember the atrocity in its detail. They were not satisfied with just killing him. Rather, they rode their horses over his body ensuring that the hooves of their Arabian steeds pounded his blessed chest. They severed his head from his body and placed his head on a spear.

They burned the tents of Imam Hussain's (a) family, knowing that all the men had been killed, except for the ailing son of Imam Hussain (a). All that remained were women and children. They terrified the children and had them running between the flames that lit the tents in that callous desert.

Every scene is more tragic and heart-wrenching than the next. The more we see the more we are shown the reality that these people's hearts were dead and their conscience lost.

Even some of the enemies themselves could not hold their tears back when witnessing some of these scenes. The enemies' ferociousness did not differentiate between young or old. Anas Al-Kahili (ra) was an elderly man who came to support Imam Hussain (a) in his movement. Because of his frail body he used to wrap his turban around his waist to help straighten his back in an effort to stand firm against the enemies. When Imam Hussain (a) looked at him, the Imam (a) cried. Anas was not spared. Mercy was not shown to young men, a nursing baby, veiled women, or little girls ei-

---

[2] Al-Muqarram, *Maqtal Al-Hussain (a)*, 272.

ther. What kind of human beings were on the other side of the battlefield and what kind of hearts did they have? They are a manifestation of the verse, *"Then your hearts hardened..."*[3]

Soldiers who stood on the other side of the battlefield themselves described the committed heinous crimes– Hameed bin Muslim, for example. As the Arabic saying goes, "With your own words, I condemn you." Another significant portion of the narrations come from the Ahlulbayt (a) whose truthfulness is undoubted by any Muslim.

Were those who committed such heinous crimes inflicted with spiritual and psychological diseases bringing them to carry out their crimes? Throughout history, in the present and the future, we will find these examples of people whose consciences are dead and hearts emptied of mercy and turned to stone. What are the reasons that caused these people to lose their humanity?

The Holy Quran points to this reality of dead and hardened hearts through a number of frank and direct verses.

Damnation is not limited to those who participated in the massacre of Imam Hussain (a) and his companions. Our pure Imams (a) supplicate to God in condemning and damning those who participated, those who were pleased, and those who followed the path of the killers of Imam Hussain (a). Take this passage from Ziyarat Warith for example, *"So, may God curse the people who killed you. And God curse the people who persecuted you. And God curse the people who*

---

[3] The Holy Quran. Chapter 2 [The Cow; Arabic: *Al-Baqara*]. Verse 74.

were pleased when they had heard of that."[4] Also in Ziyarat Ashura:

> *May God condemn and damn the people who killed you. May God condemn and damn the abettors who instigated and had a part in your murder. I turn to you and God, away from them, their henchmen, their followers and their friends. O' Aba Abdillah, I pray and invoke God to send blessings upon you. I am at peace with those who make their peace with you; I am at war with those who go to war against you, till the Day of Judgment... I ask God, who honored you above others, to be generous towards me on account of you, and give me the opportunity to be with the victorious Imam (a) from the Household of Mohammad (s)...*[5]

Those who fought Imam Hussain (a) on the battlefield had an emotional connection to the Imam (a), but that still did not stop them from killing him. There must be explanations and reasons for how the enemies killed Imam Hussain (a) in such a gruesome manner. By understanding these reasons, we can help prevent the death of moral conscience.

WHAT IS THE CONSCIENCE?

The Holy Quran ties the destiny of the human being, his personal and his social life with the movement of the individual's heart. The different positions and situations in which we found ourselves are associated with and tied to this heart. The Quran describe the various roles the heart

---

[4] Al-Shaeed Al-Awwal, *Al-Mazar*, 124.
[5] Ibid. 179.

takes and how it affects the life of the individual in each of those roles.[6]

The heart can be referred to in the spiritual aspect which God created in the human being. In it several central attributes and functionalities exist, like bravery, generosity, envy, love of others, and other attributes both positive and negative. Likewise, some positive and negative actions present themselves here like giving one the benefit of the doubt as opposed to having ill thoughts of others based on uncertain assumptions. These actions and attributes are affected by will power and freedom to choose, rising and falling, advancing and curtailing.[7]

On this basis, every time we exert effort in developing, growing and disciplining ourselves, our heart is strengthened and the positive attributes come forth. Similarly, whenever we neglect disciplining and developing ourselves, our heart experiences a decline until it reaches a state of being completely sealed, locked, or dead. From a magnanimous creation of God, we become creatures of so little worth we are valued less than animals, *"Do you suppose that most of them listen or exercise their reason? They are just like cattle; indeed, they are further astray from the way."*[8]

Our humanity is actualized through our hearts. Our physical bodies do not give us our humanity; rather, it is our heart that distinguishes us from the rest of the creation. Whenever a creation is one that holds a living conscience, a heart beating with life, filled with goodness and justice, then that

---

[6] Al-Hakeem, *Thawrat Al-Hussain (a)*, 103.

[7] Ibid. 104.

[8] The Holy Quran. Chapter 25 [Arabic: *Al-Furqan*]. Verse 44.

is a favored and honored creation. But if this conscience dies and the heart is stone, then the person is lower than animals. In fact, he is considered to be similar to an inanimate object, as the Quran describes:

> *Then your hearts hardened after that, so that they were like rocks, rather worse in hardness; and surely there are some rocks from which streams burst forth, and surely there are some of them which split asunder so water issues out of them, and surely there are some of them which fall down for fear of God, and God is not at all heedless of what you do.*[9]

HOW THE CONSCIENCE DIES

We can summarize the reasons for the death of conscience into two primary issues, from which stem a number of other topics and discussions. The two primary issues are the following: rebelling against God's will and the love of this world.

Rebelling Against God's Will

Mankind is the creation of God, created with a special and particular system. This system is peaceful and serene in its essence; however, it is subject to change and deviation. This system is what we describe as the innate nature, which the Holy Quran emphasizes protecting because it is essential to one's humanity.

> *So set your heart as a person of pure faith on this religion, the original nature endowed by God according to which He*

---

[9] The Holy Quran. Chapter 2 [The Cow; Arabic: *Al-Baqara*]. Verse 74.

originated mankind (There is no altering God's creation;
that is the upright religion, but most people do not know.)[10]

By staying in line with the boundaries and restrictions that God ordained, we are able to live by the dignity of our innate nature. We are bound to enjoy a live conscience and a calm heart. Whenever we leave these boundaries and restrictions, however, our hearts become defected. Looking back in history, we realize that the hardening of the hearts that the Children of Israel experienced was due to their refusal of and rebellion against God's laws. The Holy Quran discusses this in some of its chapters, underlining that the movement of the heart – in its rise and decline – is linked strongly to the extent of one's commitment to God's laws and restrictions. Take the following verse for example:

When Moses said to his people, 'O my people! Why do you
torment me, when you certainly know that I am God's
apostle to you?' So when they swerved [from the right path],
God made their hearts swerve, and God does not guide the
transgressing lot.[11]

Aberration and deviation from the religious guidelines result in the aberration and deviation in the movement of the heart – one can turn to the verses that discuss how the hearts are sealed and locked to expound on this point.

Note that this deviation does not take only one form, rather we observe it increase and decrease. Thus, the levels of faith, disbelief, and hypocrisy take stages and levels as well. These stages are determined by the extent of adherence, or

---

[10] The Holy Quran. Chapter 30 [The Romans; Arabic: *Al-Room*]. Verse 30.
[11] The Holy Quran. Chapter 61 [Arabic: *Al-Saff*]. Verse 5.

lack thereof, to the religious guidelines God established for us. The less we adhere to these guidelines, the greater the effect it has on our hearts. Those who went forth to battle Imam Hussain (a) transgressed in the greatest sense by eventually killing the grandson of the Holy Prophet (s). With their own free will, they rejected God's mercy. They sealed their hearts off from Divine Mercy with their own hands. The fact that these individuals chose to follow the likes of Yazid and Ibn Ziyad, fought the holy family of the Prophet – whom God ordained their love as part of the faith – and committed the most heinous crimes and gruesome acts of torture against Imam Hussain (a), collectively caused the ultimate death of their hearts, their conscience, and an undeniable mark of disgrace for humanity.

The Love of this World

The second essential issue that causes the death of the heart and the lack of conscience is indulging in the love of this world. Within this, we find immersion in its desires and pleasures, and an attachment to entertainment, money, and children away from the remembrance of God. These points evidently branch out from the fundamental issue here – the love of the world. The Holy Quran beautifully discusses this topic and the effects of the love of the world on the heart. Take the following verse:

> *Have you seen him who has taken his desire to be his god and whom God has led astray knowingly, set a seal upon his hearing and heart, and put a blindfold on his sight? So*

who will guide him after God [has consigned him to error]?
Will you not then take admonition?[12]

In another verse:

That, because they preferred the life of the world to the
Hereafter and that God does not guide the faithless lot.
They are the ones God has set a seal on their hearts, their
hearing and their sight, and it is they who are the heedless.[13]

The calm and tranquil heart is one that is not distracted
from the remembrance of God, and thus will not experience a dead conscience. Instead, that person will live in the
grace and love of God. The individual who is immersed in
the love of this world, however, will experience an ultimate
loss. The Holy Quran warns us of this reality, emphasizing
that we should not allow material and worldly things be a
reason for our distance from God and lack of obedience to
His laws. "*O you who have faith! Do not let your possessions and*
children distract you from the remembrance of God, and whoever does
that—it is they who are the losers."[14] In another verse, God says:

Say: If your fathers and your sons, your brethren, your
spouses, and your kinsfolk, the possessions that you have
acquired, the business you fear may suffer, and the dwellings
you are fond of, are dearer to you than God and His Apos-
tle and to waging jihad in His way, then wait until God is-
sues His edict, and God does not guide the transgressing
lot.[15]

---

[12] The Holy Quran. Chapter 45 [Arabic: *Al-Jathiya*]. Verse 23.

[13] The Holy Quran. Chapter 16 [The Bees; Arabic: *Al-Nahl*]. Verse 107-108.

[14] The Holy Quran. Chapter 63 [The Hypocrites; Arabic: *Al-Munafiqoon*]. Verse
9.

[15] The Holy Quran. Chapter 9 [The Repentance; Arabic: *Al-Tawba*]. Verse 24.

We must take the greatest precaution to ensure that the love of power, money, and the rest of what is associated with the love of this world, do not get the best of us. If we do not keep our guard up, we will definitely be at a loss since it will be more difficult for us to stay committed to the commandments of God.

Indulging in the pleasures and desires of this world played a major role in killing the conscience of the community, which inadvertently was transformed to a group of beasts that oppressed and killed the grandsons of the Holy Prophet (s). Take Omar ibn Saad, for example. On the Day of Ashura, after Ali Al-Akbar (a) was killed, Imam Hussain said to Omar: "... *May God sever your kin as you have severed my kin and did not honor my relation to the Messenger of God [my grandfather].*"

He, Omar, was the son of Saad ibn Abi Waqqas – the conqueror of Iraq and one who was considered to be of the companions of the Holy Prophet (s). The primary reason that led Omar ibn Saad to lead the army that killed Imam Hussain (a) was his greed. He was infatuated with the promise of Yazid to rule over the lands of 'Rey' (parts of modern day Iran). On the Day of Ashura, Omar ibn Saad launched the first arrow against the camp of Imam Hussain (a) and called out, ""Witness for me before the Prince (Yazid) that I was the first to cast his arrow!" And it was in this manner that Omar ibn Saad threw away all of principle in pursuit of his desire to rule over the lands of Rey. He became the killer of Imam Hussain (a). He ordered his soldiers to trample on his beheaded body with their horses. He caused the greatest tragedy that humanity has ever witnessed. He did this all because he sought to fulfill a worldly desire.

We must be weary of falling in the love of this world and indulging in its desires and pleasures. We must take caution and be mindful, lest we stand at a fork in the road of our journey one day and choose a path of falsehood instead of the path of righteousness.

CLASH OF FAITH IN SOCIETY

In the name of God, the most Beneficent, the most Merciful

We carried the Children of Israel across the sea, whereat they came upon a people cleaving to certain idols that they had. They said, 'O Moses, make for us a god like the gods that they have.' He said, 'You are indeed an ignorant lot. What they are engaged in is indeed bound to perish, and what they have been doing shall come to naught.' He said, 'Shall I find you a god other than God, while He has graced you over all the nations?[1]

It is easily noticeable that the Quran speaks about the Children of Israel in many of its verses. That is because in their society many exhibited contradictions, despite the many prophets and apostles that were sent to them in hopes of creating a vitreous community based on the principles of faith. No matter how many blessings God bestowed upon them, many remained ungrateful. No matter how much God honored them and favored them, many remained at-

---

[1] The Holy Quran. Chapter 7 [The Heights; Arabic: *Al-A'raf*]. Verses 138-140.

tached to this world and its material bounties and disregarded the moral and metaphysical aspects of life. Therefore, we see a great number of verses and chapters in the Holy Quran speaking of the Children of Israel. On another note, the Quran is providing us with examples of the erroneous conceptions that that society bore so that we can learn from their mistakes.

Yet, we must ask this important question: is the nation of the Prophet Muhammad (s) – the nation of Islam and the Quran – immune of these dangerous illnesses? Are we immune to the illnesses that drive mankind away from God and towards sin and deviance?

Before we answer this question, we must make clear this fact: God, the High and Glorious, does not have any special relationship to any of his creatures. *"He neither begat, nor was begotten, nor has He any equal."*[2] All of His creatures are at an equal footing in creation. It is only their sincere obedience to Him that draws some closer to him. Some, such as prophets and divinely appointed Imams, have a type of immunity, and that was earned by virtue of their sound choices and not arbitrarily granted to them by God.

We must also point out that amongst God's methods is the use of trials and tests for all of humanity so that the good can be distinguished from the evil. Therefore, tribulations that might have befallen the nations of the past may befall nations of the future. The trials experienced in other societies can become a test for our societies. We see that the Quran presents a great number of parables from the nations

---

[2] The Holy Quran. Chapter 112 [Arabic: *Al-Ikhlas*]. Verses 3, 4.

of the past so that it can warn us against falling into the same illnesses and misery that had afflicted them. One of the most severe of these illnesses is the illness of deviation away from divine values and the deterioration of human morals.

If we were to examine the reality of our lives, we would see that we are living with these dangerous illnesses that have extensive effects on our lives. How many of us teach our children the value of worldly belongings without teaching them the values of Islamic faith? How many of us rebel against noble traditions until we disconnect from even our religion? How many of us are embarrassed to practice our faith in front of others and would rather neglect religious rituals than go through that flawed sense of embarrassment? How many other examples can we think about where we neglect or abandon our faith for some worldly reason?

When we reflect on our present situation, we find a number of reasons for which we fall prey to such illnesses.

IGNORANCE

Ignorance plays a large role in this struggle, as it shields our sight from reality. When the Israelites ask, in a Quranic verse, for an idol to worship, God attributes this request to ignorance. They foolishly mixed up worshiping God and worshiping a man-made idol. An ignorant individual is not conscious of the truth and does not see reality clearly. Whoever is ignorant of where true happiness lies, and is ignorant of his true position in the world, will certainly cling to materialistic values in his actions and character. That is because materialistic pleasures are more tangible in the eyes of one with that worldview and outlook. They are the 'quick fix,' no matter how short-lived, and no matter the detrimental consequences that follow so quickly and surely.

A person who does not know the meaning of worship or the happiness that it brings and does not see the good in divine principles will certainly live a materialistic life. He will see happiness in his material wealth, worldly knowledge, and social status. We see that the majority of us will do the impossible to have our children attend the best of schools and universities so that they can live a successful and comfortable life. We see this as one of our primary responsibilities towards our children.

All of this is great for our children. But it cannot come at the cost of their true and eternal happiness. A good education and a luxurious life must not be made goals in and of themselves. They are a means to achieving happiness. But without even the simplest of knowledge in faith and ethics, all of this would be for naught. Whoever puts great efforts in providing his children with a great education in arts and sciences but does not provide them with a solid base in religious knowledge and ethics has committed a grave mistake and an offense against his children. What good would these tools for a prosperous worldly life be if we are not equipped with the tools to attain eternal happiness? Our children need an education in Quranic ethics. Parents should raise their children to exhibit virtuous characters and Quranic principles.

If our society was built on the principles of knowledge and character, it will not fall into the traps of ignorance that lead to such illnesses. We would not have put secular education at the forefront and completely disregarded any religious education. We see that God has placed a great deal of emphasis on religious education as it creates the necessary barrier against sin. Whenever a person learns more about his faith, he becomes more resilient against the influence of false precepts and deviance. Whenever a person learns the Quran and becomes tied to it, following the teachings of the religion becomes easier.

WEAKNESS

Weakness is one of the important reasons that make an individual live in a state of disharmony between the reality of life and his religious teachings. Such an individual will try to "fit in" in his environment, even at the cost of his own faith and principles. How many of us miss their mandatory prayers when they are traveling? Some may not feel comfortable praying on a plane because they feel that everyone on that plane will look down on them – and that is not the case. How many loosen their standards of modesty because the environment around them is not a modest one? How many fall into sin and deviance due to their weakness and inability to stand up to peer pressure and social pressures?

Some may reject the teachings of the religion under the guise of modernization and progress. Yet, they take only the worst that modern and progressive societies have to offer and reject the values that so-called progressive societies maintain and that coincide with our principles. If a person truly wants to be "progressive," let him abide by the standards of citizenship; let him exhibit a strong work ethic and respect the law. Rather we see that some individuals adopt the worst that modern society offers and reject all the worthy values that it adopts.

A believer should not live such a state weakness. He must have a sense of belonging and a relationship with a higher power – the absolute power of the Almighty, Honorable, and All-Wise God. We see that whenever an individual feels a sense of belonging to someone or something that is more powerful, they feel a sense of strength that comes along with that belonging. So what would a person feel when he has a sense of belonging to God, the fairest of judges, Lord of the heavens and the Earth, the Honorable, the All-Wise? How can an individual who has established a relationship to such a power ever feel weakness? *"Yet all [honor] belongs to God and His Apostle and the faithful, but the hypocrites do not know."*[3]

He describes anyone who thinks that they can attain honor by any other means by saying, *"those who take the faithless for allies instead of the faithful. Do they seek honor with them? [If so,] indeed all honor belongs to God."*[4]

There is a beautiful narration attributed to Imam Sadiq (a) describing the honor of the believers, where he says:

> *God empowered the believers in everything, except that they be dishonorable [or dishonored]. Have you not heard God's words, "Yet all [honor] belongs to God and His Apostle and the faithful"? The believer is honorable and is not dishonorable. A believer is more honorable than*

---

[3] The Holy Quran. Chapter 63 [The Hypocrites; Arabic: *Al-Munafiqoon*]. Verse 8.
[4] The Holy Quran. Chapter 4 [The Women; Arabic: *Al-Nisaa*]. Verse 139.

a mountain. A mountain can be chipped away with pick-axes, but a believer's faith cannot be chipped away.[5]

MATERIALISM

A side effect of weakness is attachment to this world and submergence in its pleasures. Whoever sees his personal benefit in this world will not bear parting with it, and will grow more and more attached to it. It will take him further away from realizing the truth of the hereafter. We see our Imams (a) indicating that *"the love of this world is at the head of every sin."*[6] It is also narrated that the Commander of the Faithful (a) said, *"love of this world ruins the mind, blocks the heart from listening to wisdom, and merits a great punishment."*[7] There are many more narrations that warn of undue attachment to this world, drawing our attention to the fact of the eternal nature of the hereafter.

This does not mean that we cannot enjoy any of the pleasures of this world and all the blessings that God has created in it. Rather, religion has called for us to enjoy the blessings of God and aim to live in comfort. The true share of value in this world lies in it being an investment into the eternal life ahead of us. When we lead our lives in this world with the right behavior and intention, whether in times of work or responsible leisure, that is a key to paradise in the Hereafter. God says:

---

[5] Al-Kulayni, *Al-Kafi*, 5:63.
[6] Ibid. 2:315.
[7] Al-Nuri, *Mustadrak al-Wasa'el*, 12:41.

Seek the abode of the Hereafter by means of what God has given you, while not forgetting your share of this world. Be good [to others] just as God has been good to you, and do not try to cause corruption in the land. Indeed God does not like the agents of corruption.[8]

---

[8] The Holy Quran. Chapter 28 [The Parables; Arabic: *Al-Qasas*]. Verse 77.

SIN

In the name of God, the most Beneficent, the most Merciful

It is narrated that the Commander of the Faithful (a) said,

> *I am amazed by how people look after what they eat in fear of illness, but they do not safeguard themselves from sin in fear of hellfire.*[1]

PERSPECTIVE

Amongst the issues that are widely agreed upon by society is the position that everyone should avoid things that cause harm to the body. Whoever rejects this is not considered reasonable, as no reasonable person would willingly subject himself to harm and illness. That is why people commonly use the idiom "prevention is better than cure." That is because a person may go through a lot of suffering to finally be cured of an illness, where all that suffering could have been averted if the illness was prevented. I do not think any reasonable person would argue against this.

---

[1] Al-Harrani, *Tohaf Al-'Oqool*, 204.

We know that human life is not limited to life in this world. Rather, mankind has been promised eternal life. The body is only a temporary means of physical activity for the everlasting soul. The body will die and the soul will remain. The soul will experience a number of different worlds until it reaches eternal bliss or punishment. Therefore, preserving the body only serves to preserve a temporary affect. Death is something that is bound to befall every person. Still, a person should look after their body so that they do not live in suffering and illness.

With all this in perspective, we must mention another point. The soul – the eternal aspect of our life – can become ill just like the body. Rather, the illnesses that befall the soul are more severe and have harsher consequences than those that affect the body. An illness that comes over the body is temporary, no matter how long it lasts; it will die out with the death of the body. However, the illnesses that overcome the soul may be everlasting just as the soul is everlasting. The most severe consequence that a disease can cause is death, which is merely a passage from one world to the next. Whereas a disease of the soul could lead to consequences as severe as an eternal abode in hellfire. Therefore, prevention of illnesses to the soul should be given greater attention than any illness that may affect the body.

Among the most important causes of these spiritual diseases are sin and deviation. As such, we should point out a few methods that will allow a person to safeguard himself from these illnesses.

Remembrance of God

First, the remembrance of God is one of the most important methods for preventing and curing these spiritual diseases. A person should live with the constant realization of God's presence and in a state of addiction to the remembrance of God. If a person's heart lives on the remembrance of God, he will not fall into sin. God's remembrance will safeguard against a number of things as it drives away Satan. And there are many narrations that emphasize this point. For example, it is narrated that Imam Ali (a) said, *"remembrance of God drives away Satan."*[2] And from the supplications of Imam Sajjad (a), *"and you made for us an enemy that plots against us… so defeat his power over us with Your authority, so that you imprison him away from us though our constant supplications and so that we are safeguarded by You from his plots."*[3]

Satan is a primary factor in the deviation of mankind and their falling into sin, but remembrance of God will drive him away. This will leave Satan no avenue by which he can whisper to an individual or drive him to deviation, making the individual safe from these sins.

In addition, a primary cause for our sin is heedlessness – that is, heedlessness and negligence of the heart. Due to heedlessness, the self begins to whisper and drive the individual into sin. Here, remembrance plays the role of bringing the self back to life and standing in the way when it may fall into heedlessness. Remembrance will allow the self to

---

[2] Al-Wasiti, *'Uyoon Al-Hikam wal Mawa'ez*, 255.
[3] Imam Zein Al-Abideen (a), *Al-Saheefa Al-Sajjadiya*, Supplication 25.

stand in the face of these whispers. It is narrated that the
Prophet (s) said:

> God said 'If I know that what overtakes a servant of Mine
> is My remembrance, I transfer his desires towards asking
> Me and conversing with Me. If My servant was such and he
> wanted to become heedless, I will intervene between him and
> heedlessness. Those are my true close servants. Those are the
> true heroes.'[4]

This is how remembrance stands in the way of the primary
causes of sin. Satan and the whispers of the self are the two
primary factors for falling into sin and deviance. Remembrance of God stands in the way of these two. It repels Satan and it does not allow a person to fall into negligence and
heedlessness.

It is through remembrance that a man may live a good life,
free of the sins that would take him to a severe punishment
and that would ruin this worldly life as well. Sin is not only a
problem for the hereafter. Rather, it has its effects on an
individual in this life as well. The Quran addressed lack of
remembrance of God and its effects on an individual:

> But whoever disregards My remembrance, his shall be a
> wretched life, and We shall raise him blind on the Day of
> Resurrection. He will say, 'My Lord! Why have You raised
> me blind, though I used to see?' He will say: 'So it is. Our
> signs came to you, but you forgot them, and so you will be
> forgotten today.'[5]

---

4 Al-Hilli, 'Uddat Al-Da'ee, 235.
5 The Holy Quran. Chapter 20 [Arabic: Ta Ha]. Verses 124-126.

Not remembering God is a cause for living a wretched life in this world, as the individual will be submerged in desires and sin that take him to a deteriorating psychological state, regardless of the punishment in the hereafter.

REMEMBRANCE OF DEATH

We see that one of the important causes for an individual's falling into deviance and committing of sins is an excess of debasing hope and a feeling that death is a distant thing. By debasing hope, I mean negative hope that hinders one's progress, making the person procrastinate and make poor choices in the present. A human being tends to get caught up in this world, behaving as if he/she will live here forever. A person who is heedless of death will seek to fulfill all of his desires, even the debasing ones, and continue to build and collect for this world as if he will live in it for eternity. A narration of Imam Sadiq (a) refers to this reality, as it says, *"God has not created anything that is so certain and without doubt, but that is perceived to be a doubt with no certainty about it, like death."*[6] Mankind lives as if death is a mere possibility, when it is in fact a certain reality and an inevitable truth. If a person is able to remind himself of this inevitability, and the prospects of retribution after death, he will without a doubt distance himself from deviance. He will be far from committing sin because he knows that this life is fleeting and that he must face the inevitable end of this worldly life, along with the permanent consequences in the hereafter.

---

6 Al-Saduq, *Al-Khisal*, 14.

So we see that God placed great emphasis on the visitation of graves and cemeteries, reflecting upon their significance, and learning from the lessons of those who have passed. Cemeteries are reminders of the inevitable end. When you visit a grave, you will realize where you will certainly end up. You will begin preparing for this new home, knowing that every moment you live is a moment closer to that transition.

The Prophet (s) emphasized the importance of remembering death because of its importance in this journey. It is narrated that he (s) said, *"intensify your remembrance of the destroyer of desires."* He was asked who this destroyer of desires is, he replied, *"Death. The best of believers is the one who remembers death the most, and who is most prepared for it."*[7]

CHOOSING FRIENDS

It is an indisputable fact that friends and companions can affect an individual in many ways. In fact, there may not be anyone who can affect an individual as much as a friend. It is narrated that Imam Ali (a) said, *"a friend is the closest of those who are close."*[8] Therefore, one of the most important causes of falling into sin is befriending people of sin and deviance. The Holy Quran stresses this truth in a number of verses, such as the following:

> *Some of them will turn to others, questioning each other. One of them will say, 'Indeed I had a companion who used to say, "Are you really among those who affirm that when we have died and become dust and bones, we shall be*

---

[7] Al-Nuri, *Mustadrak Al-Wasa'el*, Volume 2, page 100.

[8] Al-Wasiti, *'Uyoon Al-Hikam wa Al-Mawa'ez*, 50.

*brought to retribution?'" He will say, 'Will you have a
look?' Then he will take a look and sight him in the middle
of hell. He will say, 'By God, you had almost ruined me!
Had it not been for my Lord's blessing, I too would have
been among those mustered [in hell]!'*[9]

These verses give us an example of an individual who was
not influenced by his friends.

There is another example that the Quran mentions, showing
the effects of listening to bad friends:

*It will be a day when the wrongdoer will bite his hands, say-
ing, 'I wish I had followed the Apostle's way! Woe to me! I
wish I had not taken so and so as a friend! Certainly he led
me astray from the Reminder after it had come to me, and
Satan is a deserter of man.'*[10]

Moreover, the Quran tells us that friendship must be built
on a basis of piety and faith, and that would be a friendship
with lasting effects that will reach the hereafter. Every other
type of friendship will change to enmity on Judgment Day.
God says, *"On that day, friends will be one another's enemies, except
for the Godwary."*[11]

---

[9] The Holy Quran. Chapter 37 [Arabic: *al-Saffat*]. Verses 50-57.

[10] The Holy Quran. Chapter 25 [Arabic: *al-Furqan*]. Verses 27-29.

[11] The Holy Quran. Chapter 43 [The Ornaments; Arabic: *al-Zukhruf*]. Verse 67.

REPENTANCE

In the name of God, the most Beneficent, the most Merciful

[Acceptance of] repentance by God is only for those who commit evil out of ignorance and then repent promptly. It is such whose repentance God will accept, and God is all-knowing, all-wise. But [acceptance of] repentance is not for those who go on committing misdeeds: when death approaches any of them, he says, 'I repent now.' Nor is it for those who die while they are faithless. For such We have prepared a painful punishment.[1]

GOD'S MERCY

God's wisdom has dictated that His door be open for whoever wishes to reach him. He did not prohibit anyone from turning to Him and returning to obedience and worship. His mercy on his creations has dictated that He never cut off the ropes of hope to anyone until the last moments of their life so that they may come back to Him.

---

[1] The Holy Quran. Chapter 4 [The Women; Arabic: *Al-Nisaa*]. Verses 17, 18.

God is the creator of mankind. He is the one who has granted him so many blessings. His love to this servant who is His creation cannot be measured or described. He does not want anything but the best for His servants. He wants them to journey to the destination of paradise for which they were created. This paradise is theirs if they walk the path of virtue and play their role in this world as God pleases. God has therefore placed many opportunities through which an individual can attain God's pleasure. One of the greatest of these opportunities is the ability to repent. God has opened this door of mercy for His servants so they could enter it whenever they please, so long as the opportunity remains. If they take this opportunity, they gain His pleasure. As a narration of Imam Baqir (a) describes:

> God Almighty's pleasure for a servant's repentance is greater than the pleasure of a man who has lost his caravan and his supplies in a dark night and then found them. God's pleasure for the repentance of a servant is greater than the pleasure of that man who had found his caravan.[2]

REPENTANCE BRINGS CLOSURE

Committing a sin creates a form of psychological instability for the sinner. When a person rejects belief in the truth and deviates from the path, he goes against his innate nature. This person lives with a focus on worldly pursuits, sinking deeper into greed and worry over losing the limited physical pleasures. Such an individual lives in a state of anxiety, indulging in all the toxic practices this world has to offer,

---

[2] Al-Kulayni, *Al-Kafi*, 2:435.

hopelessly trying to find peace and tranquility in a turbulent sea. The more he/she drinks, the thirstier he/she gets because this water is salty. A deviant individual cannot live in psychological stability. God Almighty says, *"But whoever disregards My remembrance, his shall be a wretched life."*[3] Other verses describe the wretched life of a sinner who had gone astray from the path of God and became a slave to worldly desires. Here comes the role of repentance in restoring a state of stability and true contentment for mankind. It brings hope to a person's life, so that each individual is able to rectify his actions. An individual cannot walk on God's ordained path without the combination of hope and fear equally, so that he refrains from what harms him and is attracted to what is good for him.

Imagine that God had not opened the gates of repentance for His servants, and had decreed that whoever disobeys Him cannot return to the fold of His obedience. This may be a cause for further deviance away from his commands. Such an ideology allows for greater deviance, as each person who commits even a single sin may lose hope in God's forgiveness.

The Holy Quran comes to show us that the path of repentance is open to all, and that losing hope in God's mercy is one of the greatest sins an individual can commit. God says:

> *Say [that God declares,] 'O My servants who have committed excesses against their own souls, do not despair of the mercy of God. Indeed God will forgive all sins. Indeed, He is the All-forgiving, the All-merciful. Turn penitently to*

---

[3] The Holy Quran. Chapter 20 [Arabic: *Ta Ha*]. Verse 124.

Him and submit to Him before the punishment overtakes
you, whereupon you will not be helped.[4]

Some imagine that opening the doors of repentance justifies
future sins because they can be followed by repentance.
That is a flawed idea for many reasons. Moreover, one cannot guarantee he/she will live past the sin in order to repent. Furthermore, even if one is sure he/she will live past
the moment of sin, he/she cannot guarantee a true state of
heart in which the fire of regret can burn away the sins. Repentance is not lip-service. It is about sincere regret and a
change in one's ways.

The doors of repentance are open because of God's mercy
and wisdom. Sin is not an excuse for individuals to sin even
more, as some may think. If we break one jar, it does not
justify breaking the others. Repentance further brightens up
the dark skies for the sinful, urging them to have hope and
come back to the path of righteousness without breaking
any more jars. Otherwise, the psychological state of a sinful
person may lead him/her to despair, God forbid.

STAGES OF REPENTANCE

Repentance is the return of a servant to God. When a person sins, he leaves the circle of obedience and servitude to
God. Repentance is a return to that circle of obedience.
God says, *"Rally to God in repentance, O faithful, so that you may*
be felicitous."[5]

---

[4] The Holy Quran. Chapter 39 [Arabic: *Al-Zumar*]. Verses 53, 54.
[5] The Holy Quran. Chapter 24 [The Light; Arabic: *Al-Noor*]. Verse 31.

Some may wonder "if repentance is a return to the obedience of God, does it apply to the prophets and their immaculate successors?"

God created mankind in complete dependency in all aspects. A human cannot benefit himself or do any good independently. We are all in need of God, and we must all turn to Him. This is evident for anyone who has sinned. As for the prophets and their immaculate successors, they never choose to fall out of God's favor. They do not commit forbidden deeds. Hence, whatever we hear or read about them falls within a span of actions that God is pleased with. However, some actions are more pleasing to God than others. There may come a time where a righteous individual feels he may have distanced himself slightly from God due to his actions, and so he seeks repentance to get closer to God. But even that may not be the case. Sometimes the very nature of servitude to God Almighty makes the humble servant feel like even his best of deeds are so little before God's majesty. This drives the servant to cry out from the core of his being seeking God's forgiveness for his inherent shortcomings. This is not the same sense of repentance that an actual sinner would seek. In one verse of the Quran, God turns to Adam with special mercy. God says, *"Then Adam received certain words from his Lord, and He turned to Him clemently. Indeed He is the All-clement, the All-merciful."*[6] If this verse implies that Adam (a) was seeking repentance as well, it is surely not the repentance of a disobedient sinner but rather the repentance of one overcome by a sense of servitude, seeking more of God's favor. Adam received spe-

---

6 The Holy Quran. Chapter 2 [The Cow; Arabic: *Al-Baqara*]. Verse 37.

cial words from God – those words being the names of the Prophet Muhammad (s), the Commander of the Faithful Imam Ali (a), Lady Fatima (a), Imam Hasan (a), and Imam Hussain (a) as our narrations indicate – these would be the intercessors through whom God would bestow further favor upon Adam (a).

THE CONDITIONS OF REPENTANCE

Misdeeds through Ignorance

There are two types of sinful individuals who may outwardly seem to repent: one who is sincere and regrets his misdeeds at the very core of his being, turning to God wholeheartedly; and another who is insincere, has not really changed at heart, but puts on the act of one who turned back to God. The former individual qualifies for God accepting his repentance while the latter individual does not. God says, "*Indeed those who turn faithless after their faith, and then advance in faithlessness, their repentance will never be accepted, and it is they who are the astray.*"[7]

Furthermore, one may argue there is an indicator that implies a greater likelihood of sincerity when a person repents. This indicator goes back to the factors that drove a person to sin in the first place. There may be an individual who is otherwise one of upright character, but in a moment of heedlessness, his carnal desires get the best of him. Yes, this person may very well know that his action is sinful and that he still has the free will not to sin, but he feels weak because of the temptation. So he sins. On the other hand, there may

---

[7] The Holy Quran. Chapter 3 [Arabic: *Aal Imran*]. Verse 90.

be another individual who chooses to sin simply as a challenge to God Almighty. This individual knowingly and consciously chooses to disobey God because he belittles God's commands and chooses to take the path of evil in spite of God. Both individuals have sinned. Both are morally responsible and liable for punishment. But is there not a difference between the two? If the former individual repents, then he can cry out to God the way we see that Imam Sajjad (a) teaches us in one of his supplications,

> O' my Lord! I did not disobey You when I did because I rejected Your divinity or because I belittled Your commands or that I was daringly challenging Your punishment or that I did not appreciate Your forewarning. Yet the mistake has occurred, and my self misled me and my sinful desires won over me and my misery helped me to it and Your protective veil over my sins lured me.[8]

As for the latter individual, can he make the same claim? Would a sincere repentance ever even come out of such an individual? One thing is clear: the drive behind this person's sin seems to make it less likely that he would sincerely repent.

Haste in Repentance

Some may think that because the door of repentance is open, there is no need to hasten in repentance. They would say: so long as we have time to live on, let us take our share of the pleasures of this world, and then we will repent when we get older. This is a naive perception of repentance and it may even have a hint of mockery towards God and his

---

[8] Al-Tusi, *Misbah Al-Mutahajjid*, 589.

commands. However, *"It is God who derides them, and leaves them bewildered in their rebellion."*[9]

True repentance is the one that the person performs in sincerity, asking God for forgiveness and with full regret for his disobedience. If a person continues to sin and only turns to repentance when he is no longer able to commit that sin, we cannot always call this person repentant. He is not repentant unless he is turning back to God with sincerity and regret. Who is to say that our repentance would be truly sincere after all the rust of sins has enclosed our hearts? Who is to guarantee that we will live until the next blink of an eye such that we can delay repentance? So we cannot keep pushing off repentance. Repentance must come sincerely and soon, before it is too late. As God says

> *But [acceptance of] repentance is not for those who go on committing misdeeds: when death approaches any of them, he says, 'I repent now.' Nor is it for those who die while they are faithless. For such We have prepared a painful punishment.*[10]

---

[9] The Holy Quran. Chapter 2 [The Cow; Arabic: *Al-Baqara*]. Verse 15.
[10] The Holy Quran. Chapter 4 [The Women; Arabic: *Al-Nisaa*]. Verses 17, 18.

WHY WE SIN

In the name of God, the most Beneficent, the most Merciful

Indeed We presented the trust to the heavens and the earth and the mountains, but they refused to undertake it and were apprehensive of it; but man undertook it. Indeed he is most unjust and ignorant.[1]

We can divide mankind into two primary categories: those who have accepted God, His messengers, His Holy Scriptures, and His angels; and those who have disbelieved in God. Those who believe in God can be further classified in two categories: those who have believed in all of the messengers and all the Holy Scriptures; and those who have believed in only some of them. The Muslims are those who have believed in God, His Prophet Muhammad (s), and did not reject any of God's guidance. But we still see a great disparity between the members of this group in regards to the application of God's commands. There are those who commit sins, knowing that what they are doing is in disobedience to God and crosses the boundaries that He has drawn. *"These are God's bounds, so do not transgress them, and*

---

[1] The Holy Quran. Chapter 33 [The Parties; Arabic: *Al-Ahzab*]. Verse 72.

whoever transgresses the bounds of God—it is they who are the wrong-doers."[2] So why does a believer fall into sin? Why do we cross the boundaries that God has drawn? Why do we deviate from the path that He has shown us?

In this chapter, we wish to shed light on the reasons for which an individual might deviate from the path and commit a sin. Even though the factors may be many, we will suffice with enumerating the most important of these factors that the Quran tells us drive humans to be "oppressive" [of himself and others].

It is important to keep in mind that these factors cannot force an individual into sin, albeit these factors can make sin more or less tempting. At the end of the day, an individual has the free will to make the right choice even if that means he/she has to struggle and swim against the tides. That is why a person is held morally responsible.

IGNORANCE

The first cause of deviation and sin is ignorance. Ignorance plays a great role in drawing the individual outside the boundaries that have been set by God. This is a fact that has been emphasized by the Quran in a number of verses, including: *"Indeed he is most unjust and ignorant."*[3] So what does ignorance mean? Or what is a sinful individual ignorant of?

Ignorance of the Self

One of the main reasons that drive a person outside the boundaries that have been set by God to deviate and to

---

[2] The Holy Quran. Chapter 2 [The Cow; Arabic: *Al-Baqara*]. Verse 229.
[3] The Holy Quran. Chapter 33 [The Parties; Arabic: *Al-Ahzab*]. Verse 72.

commit sins is ignorance of his own reality and his position in this world. The individual who has full comprehension of his place in the universe will not accept for himself to cross the boundaries that God has set. Mankind is among the greatest of God's creations in His eyes. Man was the creation for which God made His other great creations prostrate towards:

> *When your Lord said to the angels, 'Indeed I am going to set a viceroy on the earth,' they said, 'Will You set in it someone who will cause corruption in it and shed blood, while we celebrate Your praise and proclaim Your sanctity?' He said, 'Indeed I know what you do not know.' And He taught Adam the Names, all of them; then presented them to the angels and said, 'Tell me the names of these, if you are truthful.' They said, 'Immaculate are You! We have no knowledge except what You have taught us. Indeed You are the All-knowing, the All-wise.' He said, 'O Adam, inform them of their names,' and when he had informed them of their names, He said, 'Did I not tell you that I know the Unseen of the heavens and the earth, and that I know whatever you disclose and whatever you conceal?' And when We said to the angels, 'Prostrate before Adam,' they prostrated, but not Iblis: he refused and acted arrogantly, and he was one of the faithless.[4]*

So Satan disobeyed God when he refused God's commands and did not prostrate to Adam. And Satan knew of the great position that God gave to mankind, and he purposely became a force of deviation for the human race – as the Quran tells of Satan's state of mind: "*Said he, 'Do You see this*

---

[4] The Holy Quran. Chapter 2 [The Cow; Arabic: *Al-Baqara*]. Verses 30-34.

one whom You have honored above me? If You respite me until the Day of Resurrection, I will surely lay my yoke on his progeny, [all] except a few."[5]

The Quran further outlines the great status that has been given to mankind in a number of verses. God says:

> *Do you not see that God has disposed for you whatever there is in the heavens and whatever there is in the Earth and He has showered upon you His blessings, the outward, and the inward? Yet among the people are those who dispute concerning God without any knowledge or guidance or an illuminating scripture.*[6]

Therefore, the position of mankind is great in the eyes of God. When someone is ignorant of this great status, he is more likely to demean himself through committing actions that are not suitable with a human being's true position and stature. Because of this ignorance, man is more likely to demean himself to the position of cattle that care only for their desires – "*They are just like cattle; indeed, they are further astray from the way.*"[7]

When an individual knows his position and his status, he is more likely to behave in a way that is befitting of that stature. Perhaps that is why we see that society condemns a person of high social status or position acting in an inappropriate manner more severely than they condemn the same actions coming from a person of lower social position. If you were to ask why one was condemned so severely and

---

[5] The Holy Quran. Chapter 17 [The Ascension; Arabic: *Al-Israa*]. Verse 62.

[6] The Holy Quran. Chapter 31 [Arabic: *Luqman*]. Verse 20.

[7] The Holy Quran. Chapter 25 [Arabic: *Al-Furqan*]. Verse 44.

the other not as severely, the reasoning that you are given is that one of a more esteemed status is held to a higher standard. A person who values his social status should act with a sense of responsibility towards his status; he should only act in a manner that befits his status.

The Quran puts a great deal of emphasis on the need for the individual to know himself, and the importance of reason and reflection in reaching self-knowledge. One will see the value of the gift that God has given and will realize that every aspect of his/her being is in utter need of God Almighty. At every level of our being, we are the property of God. When a person comes to know himself, he will act in a way that is suitable with his position. The Quranic verses that describe the concept of knowing oneself are many – among them is the verse saying, *"In the earth are signs for those who have conviction, and in your souls [as well]. Will you not then perceive?"*[8]

The Commander of the Faithful (a) emphasizes through his teachings the importance of self-knowledge and that an individual can achieve the greatest rewards through that self-knowledge. He said, "the greatest victory is attained by one who is successful in gaining self-knowledge,"[9] "whoever comes to know himself will know others more,"[10] and "whoever comes to know himself will struggle against it."[11]

---

8 The Holy Quran. Chapter 51 [The Winds; Arabic: *Al-Dhariyat*], Verses 20, 21.
9 Al-Wasiti, *'Uyoon Al-Hikam wa Al-Mawa'ez*, 497.
10 Ibid. 438.
11 Ibid. 453.

Moreover, Imam Ali (a) made clear that the path to knowing God goes through self-knowledge. He said, "whoever knows himself knows his Lord."[12]

A person that knows himself and knows his place in the world will be able to deal with anything based on that knowledge and stature, and is unlikely to knowingly take any unsuitable action. Ignorance is one of the most important factors that drive a person into deviance and sin, and self-knowledge is the method for safeguarding against this factor.

Ignorance of Consequences

The other form of ignorance that can lead a person to deviate and transgress against the boundaries that have been set by God is ignorance of the consequences of these transgressions. These consequences do not stop at the individual, but they spill over into society and even into his material surroundings. Mankind is an integral part of the wider universe. He affects and is affected by his surroundings. Each individual's actions affect him and his society, and that is a simple reaction that is understood by all. However, the Quran emphasizes the effects of an individual's actions on his physical surroundings. The Quran states, *"Whatever affliction that may visit you is because of what your hands have earned, and He excuses many [an offense of yours]."*[13] The Quran also says, *"Corruption has appeared in land and sea because of the doings of the people's hands, that He may make them taste something of what they have done, so that they may come back."*[14] Likewise, good actions have

---

12 Ibid. 430.

13 The Holy Quran. Chapter 42 [The Consultation; Arabic: *Al-Shoora*]. Verse 30.

14 The Holy Quran. Chapter 30 [The Romans; Arabic: *Al-Room*]. Verse 41.

an effect on this world. So repentance, for example, is a reason for increase in wealth and offspring and is also a cause for rainfall. God says, *"Plead to your Lord for forgiveness. Indeed, He is all-forgiving. He will send for you abundant rains from the sky, and aid you with wealth and sons, and provide you with gardens and provide you with streams."*[15]

We see that an individual's ignorance about the consequences of his actions in this world – let alone the greater consequences of these actions in the hereafter where eternity may be spent in punishment or in bliss – allows him to dare and be excessive in his sins and deviations. But if we were to realize the consequences of sins in this world, we would stand against anyone who wishes to sin and try to stop them personally. That is because the consequences of a sin do not stop at the sinner, but flow over to others around him. If we were to realize this, we would enjoin what is good and forbid what is evil on a regular basis – not only because we want to protect the individual from the consequences of his actions, but because we are defending ourselves against the overspills that might occur.

MATERIALISM

Another important factor that drives individuals towards sin is love of the world and attachment to it. As the Immaculate Imams (a) have told us, love of this world is at the root of all evil. Some level of attachment to this world is a tendency caused by a number of desires and instincts that God has created in mankind. Without a love for food, mankind may

---

[15] The Holy Quran. Chapter 71 [Noah; Arabic: *Nooh*]. Verses 10-13.

not have been able to safeguard his body from starvation. Without a sexual drive, mankind may not have reproduced especially with all the challenges of rearing children. Some level of attachment to wealth may be to provide for one's own needs as well as the needs of one's offspring. Without anger, mankind may not have been able to defend themselves, their families, and their communities. Therefore, all these instincts are imbued in man for his own good and for the good of the world surrounding him. God made the intellect the leader of these faculties and allowed it to control them so they do not become excessive. God describes the love of this world's pleasures:

> *The love of [worldly] allures, including women and children, accumulated piles of gold and silver, horses of mark, livestock, and farms has been made to seem decorous to mankind. Those are the wares of the life of this world, but the goodness of one's ultimate destination lies near God.*[16]

However, when a person allows one of these faculties to take hold of his/her life by displacing the intellect, he/she becomes very attached to this world and it becomes very hard to overcome this attachment. This creates a disturbance in the human system. This is in addition to the fact that the path to paradise in the hereafter is a path that sometimes entails struggle against these desires and faculties.

Whoever wishes for a prosperous hereafter must take a stance against debasing desires and must limit desires to the boundaries drawn by God. That involves a great deal of ef-

---

[16] The Holy Quran. Chapter 3 [Arabic: *Aal Imran*]. Verse 14.

fort, fatigue, and suffering – it is, after all, what the Prophet (s) describes as the "Greater Struggle." Indeed, falling prey to these faculties is a natural tendency of an individual acting impulsively out of physical instinct. But it is when the intellect is in the driver's seat that a free spirit realizes his/her true position in this world and struggles to live up to a higher standard than mere physical satisfaction. The Prophet (s) says, *"[the path to] Paradise is filled with troubles and [the path to] hellfire is filled with [satisfaction of] desires."*[17]

Humankind generally seeks comfort and dislikes suffering – and so we are attracted to this world and its pleasures. That is fine so long as it falls in line with the path to paradise. But when this world becomes a cause for deviation, it no longer serves its true purpose for us as moral beings, and thus we must struggle for higher principles. If we seek to satisfy our desires without heeding the consequences which do not befit the innate nature with which God has imbued us, then that is the wrong direction. If we disregard the fact that these actions do not fall in line with the order that God has ordained for the world, and we see the outbreak of war, disease, and other catastrophes as a result, then we have no one to blame but ourselves. If we fail to remind ourselves of what is greater than all of this - the punishment that God has prepared for those who transgress against the boundaries that He has drawn – then what else will wake us up?

One may ask, "if it is these faculties that make an individual lean towards being so attached to this world, then why would God instill them in the human self? Would it not be better that He would create us without these desires?"

---

17 Al-Radi, *Al-Majaẓat Al-Nabawiyya*, 387.

Earlier, we referred to the possible wisdom in having these desires to maintain human life. The key to the answer is in realizing whose actions we are questioning – God's actions. If we know God Almighty, we know that God lacks no perfection. God is beyond all weaknesses, all deficiencies. His wisdom is absolute. One may ask, "why did God not create us as angels?" The answer is the same. God's wisdom has dictated that He create a being with an intellect and with no desires, and those are the angels. His wisdom also dictated that He create a being with an intellect and desires so that these beings can overcome those desires with their intellect and become better than the angels. That being is mankind. The experience of the angels is different than that of humankind. In God's wisdom, it is best to have both types of beings exist and make them aware of God in their own distinct experience.

Therefore, we see that God emphasizes that we should not be too attached to this world and its beauties. Instead, we should live with the realization that the hereafter is better and longer-lasting. We cannot even begin to imagine the difference between the fleeting pleasures of this world and the everlasting bounties of the hereafter. We can enjoy the pleasures of this world within the guidelines God prescribes as spiritually healthy, and then for eternity we will enjoy unending satisfaction, God willing.

WEAKNESS OF THE WILL

There are many people who know that they are deviating and know the consequences of their deviance. They have heard everything covered above. But they still find themselves deep in sin. They cannot stop themselves from committing these sins. Rather they do not even try to escape this reality. They are either happy with their current situation. Or they fear others that may stop them from changing or ridicule them if they did change. Or for whatever other reason that keeps them in their wretched state. Sometimes, the individual knows he/she is in a wretched state and he/she does not like it, but he/she still sins. Why? Because, this individual simply does not choose to muster the will to do what is right.

This is compounded by the fact that daring to fall into deviance has the effect of weakening the will even further! This weakness can deprive a person of priceless opportunities. This is indicated in the narrations of the Immaculate Imams (a), such as the following narration of Imam Sadiq (a). He (a) says, *"God may deprive some of His [generally good servants] from salat al layl [in order to alert them not to fall into sin again]."*[18]

A man may be preoccupied throughout the day with seeking the bounties of this world with complete negligence of the hereafter. He will not be able to block his mind from thinking about sin. So we still see him entrenched in sin despite his constant pledges to leave them. He continues to pledge because he knows their ill effects. But he continues to fall because of his weak will.

The will that is required of a man is that he becomes determined and takes a decision to leave sin, become obedient to God, and rectify what has passed of his life. This requires a number of steps, including:

---

[18] Al-Kulayni, *Al-Kafi*, 2:272, Tr. 16.

First, refraining from committing sins, especially those that cause the loss of will. For example, scholars of ethics tell us that the sin that depletes the individual's will the most is listening to forbidden singing.[19] Many people may underestimate the gravity of this sin or try to minimize its consequences. But it has such a dangerous consequence; the loss of the will and determination to avoid deviance.

Second, worship in solitude. When an individual is alone, he will not fall into insincerity in worship, such as worshipping for the sake of attention or to gain a social status. This is especially recommended at night, when no one knows that he is worshipping. A man would worship God in solitude at night and ask God to forgive his sins, conceal his defects, and accept his repentance. At that point, God would praise this worshipper to His angels as described in some of our narrations.

Third, holding onto the Holy Prophet (s) and his Holy Household (a) as intercessors, as they are the medium and the path to God. Through them God showers mercy and guidance to the worlds. Moreover, the intercession is a reality that happens when we obey God by following them. They were the ones showing the true way to God's favor. God the Exalted has commanded us to take the path to Him – "*O you who have faith! Be wary of God, and seek the means of recourse to Him....*"[20] Furthermore, when we ask God by invoking the remembrance of these true servants of God, God may choose to forgive us and answer our prayers as a

---

[19] Al-Haidari, *Al-Tarbiya Al-Roohiyya*, 235.
[20] The Holy Quran. Chapter 5 [The Spread; Arabic: *Al-Maeda*]. Verse 35.

way to honor them, even if we would not have deserved it on our own merit.

PLEASING GOD

In the name of God, the most Beneficent, the most Merciful

When the matter is all over, Satan will say, 'Indeed God made you a promise that was true and I [too] made you a promise, but I failed you. I had no authority over you, except that I called you and you responded to me. So do not blame me, but blame yourselves. I cannot respond to your distress calls, neither can you respond to my distress calls. Indeed I disavow your taking me for [God's] partner aforetime. There is indeed a painful punishment for the wrongdoers.[1]

People often find themselves living in a state of conflict between the commands and promises of God and the promises of Satan. The promises of Satan are nothing but lies, by the words of Satan himself. In trying to implement the laws of God, one experiences hardship in opposing the whims of the self and avoiding one's adverse surroundings. Much of what Islamic law prescribes does not mesh well with the whims of the undisciplined or contaminated soul's tendencies and desires. We live in the midst of a group of re-

---

[1] The Holy Quran. Chapter 14 [Abraham; Arabic: *Ibrahim*]. Verse 22.

strictions, with every restriction facing one of our many desires. This is coupled with the challenges of meeting the demands of everyday life which is even more difficult when living in a society that does not help a person in always making righteous decisions. Rather, the individual is often faced with a society that advocates not committing to the religious law with the excuse of individual freedom. They argue that 'you only live once,' and should live life to the fullest by experiencing all the world has to offer in pleasure and desire.

With all of these challenges, it would be beneficial to address the ways that can help individuals live in accordance with what pleases God, to persist against the difficulties, and to effectively resist temptations, desires, and prohibited pleasures. Among the ways to help us in this pursuit are the following: reasoning and reflection, taking the Prophet (s) and Ahlulbayt (a) as role models, and friendship through God.

REASONING AND REFLECTION

Reasoning and reflection, or contemplation, are fundamental tools referenced in the Holy Quran. They are necessary in understanding one's strengths and weaknesses and how to navigate problems and provide solutions. The Quran considers the outcome of reasoning and reflection to be the arrival at a higher point of maturity and awareness in each situation.

> *Indeed in the creation of the heavens and the earth and the alternation of night and day, there are signs for those who possess intellect. Those who remember God standing, sitting,*

and lying on their sides, and reflect on the creation of the heavens and the earth [and say], 'Our Lord, You have not created this in vain! Immaculate are You! Save us from the punishment of the Fire.[2]

In the above verse, those being referenced reflect on the creation of the skies and the Earth arriving at the conclusion that this creation has not been made in vain or without a purpose. This creation has been made by divine wisdom; and thus, one stands from this noble realization to beseech God for protection and to keep one close to Him and away from His displeasure and punishment.

A person who reflects on God's creation and the various signs of God will come to the level of knowing God. He will feel God's greatness and understand how small he is as a creature without Him. This is an essential stage in a person's growth and advancement. It can elevate him above the calls of Satan, and allow him to transcend the status of animals that only care for fulfilling their hunger and carnal desires.

This thought is in addition to the premise that reasoning and reflection on the signs of God includes reflecting on our own selves – which is among the greatest of God's signs.

"Do you suppose that you are insignificant, while within you lies the greater universe?" These are the famous words attributed to Imam Ali (a).

All of this makes us realize the system of life and the universe, along with our role in it. We begin to differentiate

---

[2] The Holy Quran. Chapter 3 [Arabic: *Aal Imran*]. Verses 190-191.

between the highness, eminence, and greatness in the calling of God and the lowness, vanity, and indignity in the calls of Satan. Remember that Satan's goal is to bring us down to the lowest level of indignity and humiliation by calling us to disobey God and turn away from our noble purpose. When we examine some societies around the world in their systems and ways and living, we can observe advancement in technology and industry. However, with that can come the price of being indulged in materialism and an increasing trend of vanity in the culture of the community. Technological advancement is usually spearheaded by such communities, whether we like it or not, but the cost it has on the moral fabric of the society is undeniable. There is a sort of emptiness that exists in such communities that are just completely indulged in materialism, as an effect of some of their advancements. You cannot go without giving such communities their due respect for their advancement of humanity in science and technology, but at the same time we must be weary of some of the associated effects. When the goal becomes simply this world, with no sight of the hereafter, such work and advancement goes in vain and becomes utilized for illegitimate uses. Those taking that path look at life as a destination for pleasure, amusement and obscenity. That perspective is coupled with the belief that a person should not be tried, challenged or tested with tribulation. This results in the individual hurting himself and possibly hurting the people around him. When God, the hereafter, and accountability for one's actions are removed from the equation of life – the outcome is not promising.

Thus, contemplation plays a fundamental role in bringing us to understand our relationship with God. It opens our eyes to realize the necessity in following God's prescription for us in obeying his guidelines and refraining from his prohibitions. Therefore, contemplation stands amongst the greatest forms of worship in proximity to God, because it is the gateway to other specific acts of worship and delving deeper into understanding God. There are a number of narrations that discuss its significance as follows:

Imam Al-Rida (a) said, "*Worship is not simply praying and fasting; rather, worship is contemplating about God.*"[3]

The Commander of the Faithful (a) said, "*Contemplation calls for righteousness and acting upon it.*"[4]

Imam Al-Hassan (a) said, "*I advise you with piety and contemplation, for contemplation is the parent (cause) of every good thing.*"[5]

TAKING THE PROPHET (S) AS A ROLE MODEL

The secret to the success of any theory is the practical implementation of that theory or vision. Many can put forward a theory of rules and values for people to follow, but such a system will not come to fruition without actual implementation. It goes without saying that the one who legislates such a system would need to be the first to commit to its rules and values. If not, then why would anyone else be expected to adhere to such a system?

---

[3] Al-Kulayni, *Al-Kafi*, 2:55.

[4] Al-Kulayni, *Al-Kafi*, 2:55 .

[5] Al-Rishhari, *Mizan Al-Hikma*, 3:2463.

One of the fundamental reasons for the success of Islam was its proposition in coherent ideas, rules, and values. Even more essential to that was the individual who came forward with the message of Islam, as he adhered to every tenet of the faith in all of its detail and specification. Thus, there was no plausible excuse to refuse adopting the vision of Islam and its divine regulations, because the human representative of the religion, with his free will, perfectly modeled his behavior for the people to follow. The Holy Prophet (s) and the Immaculate Imams (a) held this perfect essential standard in leading the people through action and adhering firmly to every code of God. The Holy Quran calls us to take the Prophet (s) as our example, *"There is certainly a good exemplar for you in the Apostle of God—for those who look forward to God and the Last Day, and remember God much."*[6]

Some may come forward and say the following: The Prophet (s) and the Immaculate Imams (a) are infallible and are unable to fall into sin. Thus, we cannot be like them and act as they did.

In answering this objection, it is important to consider the following points:

First, the individuals chosen to be Prophets (s) and Immaculate Imams (a) are not forced robots. They have the ability and free will to choose their course of action. They may choose to act, and they may not. Essentially, it is up to them, as it is in the case of all beings with free will. However, in God's eternal knowledge and wisdom, He knew that these individuals were the best of His servants, for when

---

[6] The Holy Quran. Chapter 33 [The Parties; Arabic: *Al-Ahzaab*]. Verse 21.

tested they would exercise their free will best of all. For that qualification, God chose them and protected them with profound knowledge. As such, they see the reality of sins to be so hideous that they would never choose to commit them. They are humans, facing similar challenges as other humans face, but they freely make the best choices. The fact that God chose them reveals to us that they do not fall into sin. But God would not have chosen them without the knowledge and wisdom that they were the ones qualified on their own merit, with their own free will, as opposed to everyone else.

This is one way of thinking of it.

Second, it is not expected of us to be just like the Prophet of God (s) in every aspect. It is not even possible for us to reach the status of the Prophet (s) and the Immaculate Imams (s), for no matter what we reach, we reach it by following their example, and thus they remain a step ahead of us. God chose them. They are the standard. What is expected, however, is that we take them as our role models and their lives as a template for us to follow. The Imams (a) acknowledged that others would not be able to reach their degree of devotion. For example, the words of the Commander of the Faithful (a) tell us:

> *Remember that every follower has a leader whom he follows and from the effulgence of whose knowledge he takes light. Realize that your Imam has contented himself with two shabby pieces of cloth out of the (comforts of the) world and two loaves for his meal. Certainly, you cannot do so but at*

*least support me in piety, exertion, chastity and upright-
ness...*[7]

Thus, what is expected of us is to conduct ourselves as best as we can in accordance with the path of the Immaculate Prophet (s) and Imams (a).

Third, our Immaculate Prophet (s) and Imams (a) were able to raise a group of companions who embodied the greatest traits of excellence in worship and asceticism in the world. Take for example Salman Al-Farisi, Abuthar Al-Ghafari, Ammar ibn Yassir, Miqdad, and others of the noble companions. Even if we are unable to reach a status close to the status of the Immaculate Imams (a), then it may be still plausible for us to reach a level close to the levels of Salman, Abuthar, Ammar and Miqdad. These individuals were not the chosen Immaculate Imams; nonetheless, they reached the success they attained through their hard work and dedication to obeying and pleasing God.

In summary, taking the Holy Prophet (s), Ahlulbayt (a), and their righteous companions as our role models has a huge role in helping us fully commit to the standard to which God holds us. Moreover, when we delve into the stories of their lives we can find a true guide for us on our journeys in the examples they set.

GOOD FRIENDS

Friendship has a tremendous effect on the life of the individual. The people we befriend and with whom associate have a definite influence on the way we lead our own lives.

---

[7] Al-Radi, *Nahj Al-Balagha*, 3:70, Letter 45.

This reality is one that Islam identifies and acknowledges. Not only do friends influence and affect us, but our characteristics and morals can be known by simply looking at the friends we have.

Another reality to acknowledge is the fact that the path to God is one accompanied by tests, trials, hardship, and tribulation. Sure, the resulting value of eternal bliss and potential closeness to God Almighty is more than worth it. But even if we lose focus of that, when we live out our lives in the company of righteous people, these hardships can be easier to overcome.

When we go back to the Holy Quran and the noble traditions, we notice that God emphasizes that we choose righteous friends and brothers that help us adhere to God's law. Similarly, God warns us of the consequences of taking dishonorable friends – which could be a reason for a person's punishment in hell. The following verse describes the grief and regret of the one who had a wanton and vile friend, *"It will be a day when the wrongdoer will bite his hands, saying: I wish I had followed the Apostle's way! Woe to me! I wish I had not taken so and so as a friend!"*[8]

God illustrates to us the alternative situation where a person who is a believer had a bad friend, but by God's grace that person was not corrupted:

> *Some of them will turn to others, questioning each other. One of them will say, 'Indeed I had a companion who used to say, "Are you really among those who affirm that when we have died and become dust and bones, we shall be*

---

[8] The Holy Quran. Chapter 25 [Arabic: *Al-Furqan*]. Verses 27-28.

*brought to retribution?'" He will say, 'Will you have a
look?' Then he will take a look and sight him in the middle
of hell. He will say, 'By God, you had almost ruined me!
Had it not been for my Lord's blessing, I too would have
been among those mustered [in hell]!'[9]*

From these verses we see the significant influence our
friends can have on our misdeeds. Our narrations in turn
call us to befriend righteous people and take brothers as
friends through God, because a friend through God will
help us on the path to God. This is a person whom we befriend on the basis of the principles God wants for us. Our
friendship through God is thus a friendship with one recognizing these principles and striving to achieve them for
the sake of getting closer to God. A friend through God
reminds us of God, especially if we forget Him, and supports us in contemplating about God.

Imam Ali (a) said, *"Befriend intellectuals, sit with scholars, and
defeat your carnal inclinations, and thus you will be in the company of
the friends of God."*[10] He also said, *"The greatest goodness and
righteousness is in befriending people of understanding and prevention
(of sin)."*[11]

Imam Al-Sadiq (a) said, *"Look and see those who do not bring you
closer to your religion; do not hold them in high regard and do not desire those people's companionship. For everything other than God is
perishing and abysmal in its end."*[12]

---

[9] The Holy Quran. Chapter 37 [Arabic: *Al-Saffat*]. Verses 50-57.

[10] Al-Rishhari, *Mizan Al-Hikma*, 2:1584.

[11] Al-Wasiti, *'Uyoon Al-Hukm wal-Mawa'ez*, 112.

[12] Al-Qummi, *Qurb Al-Isnad*, 51.

God points to this when he says, "*On that day, friends will be one another's enemies, except for the Godwary.*"[13]

---

[13] The Holy Quran. Chapter 43 [The Ornaments; Arabic: *Al-Zukhruf*]. Verse 67.

PIETY

In the name of God, the most Beneficent, the most Merciful

Look! The friends of God will indeed have no fear nor will they grieve – those who have faith and are [pious]. For them is good news in the life of this world and in the Hereafter. (There is no altering the words of God.) That is the great success.[1]

THE MEANING OF PIETY

Speaking of piety is very difficult, as we cannot encompass all that can be said about it in a single sermon or book. That is especially true given the fact that God has placed unparalleled emphasis on the issue of piety, due to its great significance.

Before we enter into the topic, we should tackle a number of points:

First, mankind was not created to simply move out of existence after a period of time. Rather, mankind was created to live on beyond this physical life. It is narrated that the

---

[1] The Holy Quran. Chapter 10 [Jonah; Arabic: *Younus*]. Verses 62-64.

Prophet (s) said, *"you were not created to cease to exist, rather you were created to subsist. You are simply moved from one realm to another."*[2] The true happiness or suffering of an individual depends on how he behaves, and his actions are the cause for where he ends up in the hereafter. He is either wretched in this world and the next, or he attains excellence in both of them.

Secondly, an individual cannot reach a state of happiness and bliss except by acting in accordance with a set of general guidelines. These guidelines determine the path that a person takes and his destination. A society may try its best and use reason and experimentation to put in place guidelines, processes, and laws that it hopes will achieve happiness for all. However, due to the shortsightedness and the inexperience of the human race, we constantly fall into catastrophic errors. You may pass a law today only to find out after some time the grave errors that it contains. This is normal in the course of human existence. Mankind is not capable of understanding all the details of life, and that allows for the constant error. Even if a society accomplishes the mission of placing an adequate set of standards for physical wellbeing, those standards will only encompass life in this world and will not extend to the hereafter because of our profound ignorance about that world. How many laws we see implemented that may be beneficial for this world, but are a plague for the spiritual life of the community?

Thirdly, all manmade laws must be executed in some way. The official human executive system is never able to implement the laws to their fullest extent, despite the power

---

[2] Al-Saduq, *Al-'Itiqadat fee deen Al-Imamiyya*, 47.

and authority it may have. The executive authority cannot make everyone within society respect and obey the law. The greatest countries in the world today, with all their power, resources, institutions, technology, and methods are unable to eliminate crime. Murder is rampant. Drugs are widespread. Many people still break the law, if not in public then at least in private.

This does not mean these institutions are weak or have failed. There is a missing link in these systems. This missing link is what we refer to as virtue – a disposition to behave in the right way and to maintain a moral character. This virtue is what stops corruption and oppression. Virtue must be transformed from an abstract concept to concrete characteristics embedded in members of the community. This would allow the community to see the truth and respect humanity, justice, dignity, mercy, sacrifice, and other benevolent characteristics that man can carry. It is these characteristics that allow individuals and the community as a whole to live a life of excellence.

Fourthly, virtuous character alone does not lead to true happiness in the afterlife. Rather, it must be coupled with an understanding of monotheism – the belief that the world has One Eternal Lord who is omniscient and omnipotent. He created things in the best of manners, but not because He is in need of them. He is the All Sufficient, the Independent. He will call mankind back to Him for judgment. He will reward the benevolent amongst us for his righteous deeds. He will punish the corrupt for his corruption. We will live for eternity either in bliss or in punishment.[3]

Fifthly, if a moral character is combined with an understanding of monotheism, the individual will only aspire for God's pleasure. The individual would seek to walk the path that God has created for him, because he knows that God:

1. Has no dependency whatsoever, yet all need Him. *"O mankind! You are the ones who stand in need of God, and God—He is the All-sufficient, the All-laudable."*[4]

2. The laws and codes set by God are put in place in the best interest of mankind, in this world and the hereafter. *"If you do good, you will do good to your [own] souls, and if you do evil, it will be [evil] for [your soul as well]."*[5]

3. There is no doubt that mankind will reach true happiness through following these laws that are set by God and not deviating away from them. This is because the source that put them in place cannot make a mistake. He is all encompassing of this world and the next. His is omniscient and knows the best interest of every individual. Indeed, He is the All Compassionate and All Merciful. He is more interested in their happiness than they are.

This shows us the importance of piety and why God stressed it so often.

---

[3] Al-Haidari, *Al-Taqwa fee al-Quran*, 32.

[4] The Holy Quran. Chapter 35 [The Originator; Arabic: *Fatir*]. Verse 15.

[5] The Holy Quran. Chapter 17 [The Ascension; Arabic: *Al-Israa*]. Verse 7.

Piety, then, is what protects an individual from what may cause punishment. This means not only refraining from everything that is forbidden, but refraining from some things that are permissible in and of themselves as well. As the narration states *"The permissible is evident and the forbidden is evident. But whoever plays on the edge will surely fall over [into the forbidden]."*[6]

Someone might ask, "why do we teach people to be afraid of God? Would it not be better to have people worship God out of love and not fear? Would it not be better to live a life full of hope and happiness without fear of anything?" The answer to this question is two-fold.

Firstly, love is a principle that has a great importance within the system that we outlined above. It allows people to accept God's commands and act in accordance with His will. Islam is a religion of love, and it depends heavily on the appeal to one's sentimental nature and connecting the individual to God through love. However, the Islamic concept of love is not a simple emotional drive that is devoid of action. Love, according to the Quran, is something that should be linked to acting as the beloved wishes, *"Say, 'If you love God, then follow me; God will love you and forgive you your sins, and God is all-forgiving, all-merciful.'"*[7]

Moreover, we find from the words of the Immaculate Imams that religion is about love. It is narrated that when someone asked Imam Baqir (a) about the love of the

---

[6] Al-Asfahani, *Mufradat Ghareeb Al-Quran*, 531.

[7] The Holy Quran. Chapter 3 [Arabic: *Aal Imran*]. Verse 31.

Household of the Prophet (s) and the role that it plays in salvation, he would reply *"is religion anything but love?"*[8]

So the sentimental and emotional aspects are among the aspects that Islam addressed. They were embodied in the command to love the Prophet (s), as he said, *"none of you has faith until I am more beloved to him than himself and my household is more beloved to him than his own household."* Love for the family of the Prophet (s) is an obligation ordained by God; He says, *"Say, 'I do not ask you any reward for it except the love of [my] relatives.'"*[9] And there are many more examples that emphasize love in obedience to God's commands.

Secondly, if the type of love mentioned above is purely emotional and does not extend into practicality then that type of love has proven to be a failure. Empty claims of love and misguided hopes for salvation do not cut it. The result of such a devaluation of religion has been widespread disobedience to the commands of God. Those with such notions have knowingly or unknowingly renounced the true values of the religion ironically, including the value of love.

Emotional love alone does not lead to the betterment of mankind. It must be coupled with a profound reverence of and lively devotion to God. An analogy that illustrates this point can be found in childrearing. Although there is a great deal of mutual love between a child and his parents, it would be a mistake for the parents to remove all forms of reverence and devotion from the child. The child must both love and honor his parents. This sense of respect and honor helps guarantee proper conduct even when love alone does

---

[8] Al-Kulayni, *Al-Kafi*, 8:80.

[9] The Holy Quran. Chapter 42 [The Consultation; Arabic: *Al-Shoora*]. Verse 23.

not cut it, such as when love is in conflict with the child's desires. Love is not always strong enough to make a child drink his medicine. An instilled sense of reverence for one's parents, a profound sense of respect and honor, can make it more likely for the child to take an action despite his desires.

Mankind overall is similar in the relationship with God Almighty. Weak emotional love alone is not likely to stop us from disobeying God's commands as we seek to satisfy our desires. There must be a sense of reverence and devotion coupled with love that will make one careful not to cross the boundaries drawn by God.

THE EFFECTS OF PIETY

As we discussed, God has put in place laws and teachings that are in the best interest of mankind. Some of this guidance may be meant mainly for this Earthly life, meaning that we see its effects directly on our lives in this world. Other commands of God may be meant mainly for the hereafter and have no apparent effect in this world. We would be tasked with these commands because this life is where we earn our place in the hereafter. Some divine commands may deal with both worlds, and their effects are observable in this world and the hereafter. If we are not able to see the effects in this world, that would be because of our own ignorance and shortsightedness. One of the things that have a great effect in both worlds is piety. It leads to true success in this world and eternal bliss in the next. God says, "*The friends of God will indeed have no fear nor will they grieve — those who have faith and are [pious]. For them is good news in the life of this world and in the Hereafter....*"[10]

There are a number of effects of piety that can be experienced in this world. We will list a few of them below.

The Good Life

One of the important effects of piety is "the good life." Piety allows you to live a good, content life in this world and the next. God says, "*Whoever acts righteously, [whether] male or female, should he be faithful, We shall revive him with a good life and pay them their reward by the best of what they used to do.*"[11]

God has promised those who are righteous a "good life," meaning that He will grant them a different caliber of life than the one they share with others. God grants them this form of life through His support, as the Quran says:

> *You will not find a people believing in God and the Last Day endearing those who oppose God and His Apostle even though they were their own parents, or children, or brothers, or kinsfolk. [For] such, He has written faith into their hearts and strengthened them with a spirit from Him. He will admit them into gardens with streams running in them, to remain in them [forever], God is pleased with them, and they are pleased with Him. They are God's friends. Look! The friends of God are indeed felicitous!*[12]

---

[10] The Holy Quran. Chapter 10 [Jonah; Arabic: *Younus*]. Verses 62-64.

[11] The Holy Quran. Chapter 16 [The Bees; Arabic:*Al-Nahl*]. Verse 97.

[12] The Holy Quran. Chapter 58 [The Argumentation; Arabic:*Al-Mujadala*]. Verse 22.

This spirit from God has been mentioned in a number of narrations, including the following narration from Imam Kadhim (a):

> God, the Exalted and Majestic, has supported the believer with a spirit from Him. This spirit will come to [his support] whenever he is righteous and pious. It departs him whenever he sins or transgresses. It is with him and it is moved joyously by his benevolence, but it subsides into the earth when he transgresses. Servants of God, look after God's blessings by reforming yourselves, and you will elevate in your certainty [of the truth], and you will attain a most valuable treasure. May God have mercy on a person who is on the verge of doing good and does it, or who is on the verge of doing evil but abstains from it.[13]

The good life is not about physical luxury, wealth, or satisfaction of desires. It is a life of peace, tranquility, and true happiness that most people lack. Among the most widespread ailments today are those of anxiety and stress, despite the technological advances and widespread luxuries in many parts of the world. Many people do not enjoy a good life. Rather, they live a life of despair and face the pain of psychological ailments.

On the other hand, a pious believer lives a good life that is filled with contentment with what God has given. He is truly content deep down even if tragedies and catastrophes befall him. The pious believer lives a higher caliber of life, one with knowledge and ability to see reality as it truly is. This believer differentiates between that which truly lasts forever,

---

13 Al-Kulayni, *Al-Kafi*, 2:268.

and that which perishes moment by moment. The believer's heart turns away from that which perishes and latches on to his True Lord. Then this person only wishes to be near God and only fears to be distant from God. The pious believer finds himself enjoying a pure, everlasting life, cared for completely by His Caring Lord. This believer sees the beautiful masterpiece of the Benevolent Creator. Nothing is ugly except what God sees as ugly – committing sins.[14]

We all long for this life that saves us from anxiety, stress, and fear of the unknown. And the reason for this despair is evident – it is the unwillingness to remember God. God says, *"But whoever disregards My remembrance, his shall be a wretched life."*[15]

Knowledge

Scholars of logic categorizes knowledge into two types: acquired and presential. There are a number of differences between the two categories. One important distinction is that with acquired knowledge one knows reality through a mental image. This mental image is gained by an individual through the process of learning. With presential knowledge, on the other hand, one knows reality directly. The person senses, feels and is aware of the reality in question directly, because that reality is present to the individual. This type of knowledge is not attained through a process of learning, for it is not a thinking mechanism. One example of this type of knowledge is sensing my hunger while I am hungry. Another example is sensing my own presence. Presential knowledge is about feeling/sensing my own presence or

---

[14] Al-Tabatabaei, *Tafsir Al-Mizan*, 12:342.
[15] The Holy Quran. Chapter 20 [Arabic: *Ta Ha*]. Verse 124.

something present to me. However, right when I think of that feeling as an idea, through a mental image, it is acquired knowledge, not presential knowledge.

One of the effects of piety appears in knowledge. Piety has an impact on one's insight. God says, *"Be wary of God and God will teach you."*[16] God also says, *"O you who have faith! If you are wary of God, He shall appoint a criterion for you, and absolve you of your misdeeds, and forgive you, for God is dispenser of a great grace."*[17] While this may be related to presential knowledge, as we will hint later, it clearly has an impact on one's acquired knowledge at the very least. Indeed, piety removes the dark barriers of lowly desires and worldly temptations from one's heart, allowing a person to see the truth with greater clarity upon contemplation. Piety allows a person to taste the pleasure in a deeper awareness of reality and sheds light on the guaranteed routes to achieve the sacred goal of getting closer to God Almighty. Piety, thus, leads a person to awareness and clarity.[18]

The word "criterion" in the above verse was translated from the Arabic *Furqan*, which means differentiating and discerning between matters. In this context, the "criterion" is that which distinguishes between righteousness/truth and falsehood, whether that be in beliefs – proper faith vs. deviant beliefs – or in actions – good/obedience vs. evil/sin. A pious person will not fall prey to confusion between what is true and what is false, especially when it comes to faith. The pious individual will be strong in faith and in applying the

---

[16] The Holy Quran. Chapter 2 [The Cow; Arabic: *Al-Baqara*]. Verse 282.
[17] The Holy Quran. Chapter 8 [The Spoils of War; Arabic: *Al-Anfaal*]. Verse 29.
[18] Al-Shirazi, *Al-Amthal*, 18:97.

faith. He will discern between what is good and what is wicked.

If a person has piety, the barriers of lowly desires and worldly hopes will be removed. Then a person will see clearly that he/she must learn his/her obligations further. This will drive a person to learn the laws on transactions and differentiate between which dollar is legitimate and which is not.

As for the reality of the dollar beyond the believer's responsibility, that is a different issue. Does piety lead to such knowledge of the reality? If yes, where is the evidence of that? If no, then do all of those without such knowledge lack piety? That is far-fetched.

Yes, there may be a certain caliber of piety that has different effects, such as being aware of some of the unseen. That is subject to God's wisdom. But this does not mean that without such an effect one lacks piety altogether.

According to some scholars, knowledge from piety can be of an even higher caliber than described earlier. This is knowledge that cannot be attained through studying books or through experimentation. Rather, the soul is prepared to witness this reality through profound degrees of piety that open up one's spiritual senses. The scholars who describe this say that it has been referred to in the Prophetic traditions. For example, it is narrated that the Holy Prophet (s) said, "*Each heart has a pair of eyes and a pair of ears. If God wishes good for a servant, He opens the eyes of his heart so that he sees the metaphysical [realms]."*[19]

This knowledge, then, would be of the same type that God mentions in the Quran, when He says, *"The one who had knowledge of the Book said, 'I will bring it to you in the twinkling of an eye."*[20] Or in the verse, *"[There] they found one of Our servants whom We had granted a mercy from Ourselves, and taught him a knowledge from Our own."*[21]

Escape from Troubles

An individual in this life faces a great deal of trials and tribulations. These trials and tribulations have their philosophy, and the topic could be addressed elsewhere. We will allude to a few concepts here to help explain the effects of piety. We especially want to make clear that much of the tribulations one faces go back to the individual's own misdeeds. God says, *"Whatever affliction that may visit you is because of what your hands have earned, and He excuses many [an offense of yours]."*[22]

God also says, *"And lest—if an affliction were to befall them because of what their hands have sent ahead —they should say, 'Our Lord! Why did You not send us an apostle so that we might have followed Your signs and been among the faithful?"*[23] He also says, *"So the evils of what they had earned visited them, and as for the wrongdo-*

19 Al-Haidari, *Al-Taqwa fee al-Quran,* 67. Citing: Al-Tabrizi, *Tafseer Al-Muheet,* 1:272.
20 The Holy Quran. Chapter 27 [The Ants; Arabic: *Al-Naml*]. Verse 40.
21 The Holy Quran. Chapter 18 [The Cave; Arabic: *Al-Kahf*]. Verse 65.
22 The Holy Quran. Chapter 42 [The Consultation; Arabic: *Al-Shoora*]. Verse 30.
23 The Holy Quran. Chapter 28 [The Stories; Arabic: *Al-Qasas*]. Verse 47.

ers among these, the evils of what they earn shall be visited on them and they will not frustrate [God]."[24]

There are other verses that often tell us that the causes of these tribulations go back to us. Of course, there are exceptions. Tribulations that befall a person even though he/she has committed no sin are not the ones being referenced in such verses. For instance, the tribulations that befell the Prophets (s) and Immaculate Imams (a) were meant to elevate their status even higher, not as an effect of sin, God forbid.

Sometimes we seek materialistic means to escape these trials and tribulations. Even so we may not be able to escape these troubles. But the answer is very simple. Piety is the true answer for our troubles, and not any material means that we might seek. This truth was declared by God in the Holy Quran. He says,

> *Whoever is wary of God, He shall make for him a way out [of the adversities of the world and the Hereafter] and provide for him from whence he does not count upon. And whoever puts his trust in God, He will suffice him. Indeed God carries through His commands. Certainly, God has ordained a measure [and extent] for everything.*[25]

Therefore, the means to escape troubles and difficulties are through piety. Moreover, the blessings that we account for and those that we do not account for, come through piety. This is not myth or folktales. These are the words of God. He says, and He is the All Truthful, *"and who is truer in speech*

---

[24] The Holy Quran. Chapter 39 [The Crowds; Arabic: *Al-Zomar*]. Verse 51.
[25] The Holy Quran. Chapter 65 [Divorce; Arabic: *Al-Talaq*]. Verses 2, 3.

than God?[26] I do not exaggerate when I say that many of us have gone through some sort of difficulty, at times financial and at times otherwise. We would search and search for a way out of these difficulties. It is only when we turn to God with sincerity for a few moments that a solution for the problem appears from places we would not have imagined.

Therefore, one of the most important ways to relieve yourself of troubles and difficulties is through piety. The words of the Commander of the Faithful (a) in this regard are beautiful. He says, *"if the heavens and Earth were interwoven over a servant [such that he was buried in hardship and difficulty] then he acted out of piety before God, God would create an exit for him."*[27]

Piety and the Family

Piety has a great effect on the offspring. Its effects do not stop at the individual, but may impact one's lineage – not only the direct children but even further down through the bloodline. The Quran refers to this in the verse, *"Let those fear [the result of mistreating orphans] who, were they to leave behind weak offspring, would be concerned on their account. So let them be wary of God, and let them speak upright words."*[28] This verse speaks to those who have mistreated orphans. It tells us that if we are impious in treating the orphans, the same might befall our children. To protect them, we need to be pious of God.

Impiety is a cause for troubles and difficulties for the individual and his children and grandchildren. One may ask,

---

26 The Holy Quran. Chapter 4 [The Women; Arabic: *Al-Nisaa*]. Verse 122.
27 Al-Radi, *Nahj Al-Balagha*, 2:13, Saying 130.
28 The Holy Quran. Chapter 4 [The Women; Arabic: *Al-Nisaa*]. Verse 9.

"what did the children and grandchildren do to bear the consequences of the individual's impiety?" "How could this be when God says, '*and no bearer shall bear another's burden*[29]?'"

Sin, oppression, and impiety are like diseases. They cause an illness to the individual, and the effects of this illness may be seen in the offspring, even though they are wholly innocent. Sins have an effect that is programmed in the system of creation. Much like germs may spread illness, so do sins. Knowing this should be a cause for us to be pious. A sin that we may commit does not affect us only, but it affects those who may be dearest to our hearts – our children.

Similarly, piety is a reason for safeguarding the offspring. We read in the Holy Quran the parable of the Prophet Moses (a) and the righteous servant of God.

> *So they went on until they came to the people of a town. They asked its people for food, but they refused to extend them any hospitality. There they found a wall which was about to collapse, so [the righteous servant] erected it. [Moses] said, 'Had you wished, you could have taken a wage for it.*[30]

To this question, the righteous servant answered:

> *'As for the wall, it belonged to two boy orphans in the city. Under it there was a treasure belonging to them. Their father had been a righteous man. So your Lord desired that they should come of age and take out their treasure—as a mercy from your Lord. I did not do that out of my own ac-*

---

[29] The Holy Quran. Chapter 6 [The Cattle; Arabic: *Al-An'am*]. Verse 164.
[30] The Holy Quran. Chapter 18 [The Cave; Arabic: *Al-Kahf*]. Verse 77.

cord. This is the interpretation of that over which you could not maintain patience.[31]

Piety and the Community

Nations place great importance on growing communities, developing human resources, and solving social problems. Mankind tries to solve any problem through empirical sciences. We do not reject the fact that empirical sciences have played a great role in the advancement of humanity. However, all these technological and scientific advances have not put a stop to social problems, destruction, climate change, and food and water shortages. With all its advancements, science cannot solve all of humanity's problems.

The Quran gives us the ideal answer to all these problems. The solution is piety. *"If the people of the towns had been faithful and [pious], We would have opened to them blessings from the heaven and the earth. But they denied; so We seized them because of what they used to earn."*[32]

---

[31] The Holy Quran. Chapter 18 [The Cave; Arabic: *Al-Kahf*]. Verse 82.

[32] The Holy Quran. Chapter 7 [The Heights; Arabic: *Al-A'raf*]. Verse 96.

TESTS AND TRIALS

In the name of God, the most Beneficent, the most Merciful

If wounds afflict you, a like wound has already afflicted those people; and We make such vicissitudes rotate among mankind, so that God may ascertain those who have faith, and that He may take witnesses from among you, and God does not like the wrongdoers.[1]

TRIALS AS A DIVINE METHOD

Trials and tribulations are among the divine methods that have been surrounding humanity since their first days on this Earth. No one was safe from them. Whether a divine prophet, a righteous believer, or a sinful nonbeliever, all of humanity must pass through these trials. Creation is based around these trials and tribulations, as they are the means that God has set for the refinement and filtering of each individual's heart and soul. God tests us on whether we obey his commands or disobey them. Everything in this world of life and death, wealth and poverty, health and ill-

---

[1] The Holy Quran. Chapter 3 [Arabic: *Aal Imran*]. Verse 140.

ness, youth and ageing, all were set as tests for mankind. It is these tests that separate between good and corrupt individuals. The level of tribulations is tied to the level of faith that the person has in his heart. The more a person believes, the harder the trials. An individual's state in the hereafter is decided in this world, and it differs from one person to the other. It is determined through these trials and tribulations. This relationship between belief and trials is evident in the narrations of the Immaculate Imams (a). It is narrated, for example, that Imam Sadiq (a) said, *"the individuals that face the most intense tribulations are the prophets, then those that follow them [in rank], then the next best followed by the best after that."*[2]

Even by earthly standards, this is a normal phenomenon. The individual who wishes to take on an important or notable position must pass a number of examinations to which others may not be subjected. The higher the position, the more necessary the qualifications. For example, a person must pass a number of exams and acquire some level of experience before being licensed as a physician. The same idea applies to the system created by God. With patience through trials and tribulations come great rewards from God Almighty. When God loves a servant, He wants that servant to gain more rewards, so He tests the servant with these trials and tribulations to gain the greater rewards.

A PROBLEM AND A SOLUTION

Some may ask, "a person has to go through an examination because the other side does not know what this person

---

[2] Al-Kulayni, *Al-Kafi*, 2:252.

knows. It is a method for me to determine the capacity of a person when I do not know what his capacity is. But God does not need to examine us because He is Omniscient – he knows how we would do in these examinations. So why test us? And why test His prophets and his most righteous servants?"

The answer can be seen in Imam Ali's (a) words. He explains the following verse, *"your possessions and children are only a test,"*[3] he says:

> *The meaning of the verse is that He tests them with wealth and children to identify those who are ungrateful for the blessing and those who are content with their sustenance. Even though He knows them better than they know themselves, but [He tests them] so that the acts for which an individual deserves punishment or reward appear.*[4]

God knows that a person would freely choose good or bad, and thus deserve reward or punishment. In this line of thinking, then, the person would not deserve the punishment, for instance, until he/she actually chooses the bad with his/her own free will. The tests to which God subjects an individual are not meant to fill a void in God's knowledge about the extent of that individual's faith and good deeds. Rather, they are so that the connection between deserving His reward and punishment and between the individual's deeds becomes apparent. God knows the human self better than the individual knows himself. He does not need to be shown anything – He is exalted far beyond such a claim. Rather, any trial or test is meant to give each indi-

---

[3] The Holy Quran. Chapter 8 [The Spoils of War; Arabic: *Al-Anfal*]. Verse 28.
[4] Al-Radi, *Nahj Al-Balagha*, 4:21.

vidual a grade he/she deserves as compared to all others. When a crime is committed, for instance, that is when the specific punishment for that crime is deserved. Similarly, when an accomplishment is actually made, that is when the specific reward for that accomplishment is deserved. God is the All-Just. Otherwise, each individual would argue against God when he sees that God has punished him/her for an evil that he/she did not actually commit! Therefore, God created these tests so that we can compete amongst ourselves for reward or punishment.

TRIALS AND THEIR EFFECTS

There are a number of effects that are connected to the trials of this world. If we understand these effects, we will reach the realization that trials and tribulations are a blessing from God, opportunities to be successful in overcoming these tribulations and passing these tests.

Tribulations are an Honor

When we go back to the narrations of the Holy Household of the Prophet (s), we see in their words an indication that tribulations are an honor that God grants only to the believers. The problem is that many of us think that God does not honor any of us. We do not draw the connection between His love towards us and all the blessings He grants us through trials. We also do not see that when God grants us material objects, that can sometimes be an occasion for us to show our true colors – colors that may be dark and ugly, God forbid.

It has been attributed to Imam Sadiq (a) that the Prophet Muhammad (s) said:

> ... *And God has not praised any of His servants from the time of Adam (a) to Muhammad (s) except after putting him through trials, and having the servant fulfill his obligation of servitude towards Him. Hence, the honors of God [that He bestows on His servants], in reality are the ends - the beginnings of which are tribulation...*[5]

It is also narrated that Imam Sadiq (a) said:

> *God, in His Honor and Glory, has servants on Earth who are the most sincere of His servants. Whatever precious gifts descend from the heavens, He diverts away from them. Whatever tribulation is ordained, He diverts towards them.*[6]

It is from this perspective that we understand the words of Lady Zeinab (a) as she was speaking in the courtyard of Yazid. She explains this truth in her words as he gloats in what he perceives to be a victory over Imam Hussein (a). She said:

> *O Yazid! Do you think that we have become humble and despicable owing to the martyrdom of our people and our own captivity? As you have blocked all the paths for us, and we have been made captives and are being taken from one place to another, do you think that God has taken away his blessings from us? Do you think that by killing the godly persons you have become great and respectable and the Almighty looks at you with special grace and kindness?*

---

[5] *Misbah al-Shariah*, 184 (Attributed to Imam al-Sadiq (a)).

[6] Al-Kulayni, *Al-Kafi*, 2:253.

For this reason and on account of this incorrect thinking you have become elated and arrogant. You have become boastful because you have seen that the matters have taken a turn in your favor. You have, however, forgotten what God says:

'Let the faithless not suppose that the respite that We grant them is good for their souls: We give them respite only that they may increase in sin, and there is a humiliating punishment for them.[7] [8]

Thus, one must understand the morals of this reality that Lady Zeinab (a) mentioned, and which the narrations of the Holy Household (a) have emphasized. Simply seeing that one person has been given more material benefits than the other or that one nation is more materialistically prosperous than another does not mean that the ones who have been given more are closer to God. Rather, a reasonable individual, if he sees that he is living a well-off and luxurious life without any trials and tribulations, should realize that he has distanced himself from God. God is generous with all his servants. If a person is undeserving of the rewards of the hereafter, and seeks out the pleasures of this world, then God will not deprive him of the pleasures of this world. The Quran actually tells us that if it was not for the fact that believers may be led astray by envy or other vices, God would have given more to the nonbelievers in this world. God says:

Were it not [for the danger] that mankind would be one community [all being led astray], We would have made for

---

[7] The Holy Quran. Chapter 3 [Arabic: *Aal Imran*]. Verse 178.
[8] Al-Majlisi, *Bihar Al-Anwar*, 45:133.

*those who defy the All-beneficent, silver roofs for their houses
and [silver] stairways by which they ascend, and [silver]
doors for their houses and [silver] couches on which they re-
cline, and ornaments of gold; yet all that would be nothing
but the wares of the life of this world, and the Hereafter is
for the [pious] near your Lord.[9]*

So with this understanding of the verse, if it was not for the
fact that the believers may be tempted into disbelief, God
would have given the unbelievers — out of His generosity —
houses of silver and other materialistic objects. But all of
this would fade at death and the unbeliever would be trans-
ported to an eternal abode in hellfire, experiencing the dark
reality that he/she brought upon him/herself.

Tribulations are a Reminder

We live in this world in a state of constant struggle to fulfill
our needs and not succumb to our desires. We struggle to
stay within the boundaries that have been drawn for us by
God. Even the believer lives in this state of struggle that the
Prophet (s) called "the Greater Struggle." At many times,
we find ourselves following our desires and taking comfort
in the materialistic pleasures of this world. We try to fulfill
all of our whims and desires, as we grow farther and farther
away from God. The relationship between our negative attachment to this world and our connection with God is an
inverse relationship. The more we become attached to and
fixated on this world, the farther we distance ourselves from
God. So God — the All Kind, All Compassionate, and All
Merciful — is kind enough to grant us reminders in the form

---

[9] The Holy Quran. Chapter 43 [The Ornaments; Arabic: *Al-Zukhruf*]. Verses 33-
35.

of tribulations. They allow us the opportunity to come closer to Him. God describes how He deals with some who go astray in the verse, *"We shall surely make them taste the nearer punishment prior to the greater punishment, so that they may come back."*[10]

God, in His mercy, grants us the opportunity to go back to Him. He tests us with tribulations that are meant to remind us and bring us back to the path of God. God uses these tribulations to allow us to escape the punishment of the hereafter, which cannot be compared to any other punishment. The pains of this world are nothing compared to the punishment of the hereafter.

This reality was also explained by the Commander of the Faithful (a) in some detail, when he said:

> *God tests his servants with tribulations when they act wrongly by decreasing their crops, constraining blessings, and sealing the coffers of [His] bounties. [He does so] so that whoever is willing to repent may repent, whoever is willing to journey [away from deviance] may make the journey, whoever is willing to remember may remember, and whoever is willing to be deterred may be deterred."*

Therefore, the wisdom behind these trials and the great effect of the tribulations are bringing us back to the path of God. They are to remind us of His great blessings upon us. So that whoever wishes to journey away from sin and deviance can embark on that journey. This is the great blessing that comes with any tribulation.

---

[10] The Holy Quran. Chapter 32 [The Prostration; Arabic: *Al-Sajda*]. Verse 21.

Trials are a Filter for Our Deeds

Trials are also a means by which our deeds are filtered. Mankind is a sinful race. If God wanted to judge us based on every single one of our actions, only a small number of people would find salvation. The most righteous would be saved and the rest would all be taken to hellfire. However, God, in His love and compassion towards His servants, wishes to ease the load of these sins on us through tribulations in this world. There is an amazing narration by Imam Sadiq (a), narrated to us by Yaqoub bin Younes. He says:

> *I heard Jaafar ibn Muhammad (a) say,* "Indeed damned is a body that is not afflicted every forty days." *I asked,* "damned?" *He answered,* "damned!" *When he saw the great impact that his words had on me, he said to me,* "Oh Younes! Affliction may be a scratch, jab, stumble, catastrophe, leap, the tearing of a shoe, or something similar. Oh Younes, a believer is dearer to God than to allow forty days to pass without his sins being sifted away, even if it was with a bout of sadness for which he does not know the cause. By God! One of you would put Dirhams in his hands and weigh them to find them lacking. He would be worried by that. Then he would weigh them again to find that it is the correct amount. This would be a cause for the release of some of his sins."[11]

---

[11] Al-Nuri, *Mustadrak Al-Wasa'el*, 2:59.

Trials Allow us to Rise in Status

Excellence and ascension to reach closer to God are the goals of a believer, which he will pursue throughout his life. Mankind lives in dependency and weakness. Whenever an individual ascends in closeness to God, he gains greater levels of excellence. Trials play an important role in an individual's journey towards excellence and closeness to God. When a man is faced with tribulation because of his misdeed, it is a sign for him to back off such an action. It helps alert the person to move toward an act of excellence as opposed to a state of falling into sin. The prophets and the righteous believers are faced with trials as a means for them to rise in status. This is why prophets are the ones who are confronted with the most difficult tribulations, then the righteous believers, then others in accordance to their similarity to the prophets. Whenever a person rises in status with God, the more tribulations he will face, allowing him to rise further in status. One of the companions of Imam Sadiq (a) says:

> *I asked Abu Abdillah (a) about God's words* "Whatever affliction that may visit you is because of what your hands have earned."[12] *Do you think that the tragedies that befell Ali (a) and his household are due to what their hands have earned, when they are the Immaculate Household of Purity? He said,* "The Messenger of God (s) would repent to God and ask for His forgiveness a hundred times a day, while he was without any sin. God singles out his close servants for

---

[12] The Holy Quran. Chapter 42 [The Consultation; Arabic: *Al-Shoora*]. Verse 30.

tribulation and rewards them for it without any guilt on their part. "[13]

DEALING WITH TRIBULATIONS

Knowing that trials are a divine method that befall believers, we should still pray and supplicate to God and ask for health on all levels and ask that tribulations that would harm our faith be driven away. This is because we may not be able to pass the trials that are sent our way, so we ask God not to subject us to them. However, if a person is faced with trials and tribulations, he should not be hopeless or go outside the bounds that were drawn by God. Instead, he should submit to the will of God and pray that He repel these tribulations and grant him health and safety. He should know that any ordeal has a resolution, and that difficulties are mixed with ease and blessings that will come to him. That is the express meaning of the verse, *"Indeed ease accompanies hardship. Indeed ease accompanies hardship."*[14] God asks us to endeavor towards excellence despite any hardship, adversity, or setback. As He says in the following verses, *"So when you are done, appoint, and supplicate your Lord."*[15] After you overcome the hardship that itself contains ease and blessings, you should not slow down and forget your obligations and your goal. You should continue to tread on despite all of the hardships, as this is the path of God that we must all set as our goal and strive towards with all our effort.

---

[13] Al-Kulayni, *Al-Kafi*, 2:45.
[14] The Holy Quran. Chapter 94 [The Consolation; Arabic: *Al-Sharh*]. Verses 5, 6.
[15] Ibid. Verses 7, 8.

FEAR OF GOD

In the name of God, the most Beneficent, the most Merciful

When the Greatest Catastrophe befalls — the day when man will remember his endeavors and hell is brought into view for those who can see — as for him who has been rebellious and preferred the life of this world, his refuge will indeed be hell. But as for him who is awed to stand before his Lord and restrains his soul from [following] desires, his refuge will indeed be paradise.[1]

When we study the life of Prophet Muhammad (s) and his Honorable Household (a) – those whom God removed all impurity from – we see an underlying characteristic that they all possessed. They were all fearful of God. The Prophet (s), in his perfection and holy attributes, is the best of God's creations. Yet we see that he stands before God in fear and performs all types of worship. He would pray until his feet would get swollen, until God by His mercy told him *"Ta Ha! We did not send down to you the Quran that you should be miserable."*[2]

---

[1] The Holy Quran. Chapter 79 [Arabic: *Al-Nazi'at*]. Verses 34-41.
[2] The Holy Quran. Chapter 20 [Arabic: *Ta Ha*]. Verses 1, 2.

When we observe the lives of the Commander of the Faithful (a) and the rest of the Immaculate Imams (a), we see that they stand before God with so much fear that their faces would turn pale and their bodies would tremble. So if this is the condition of the most beloved to God and the closest creations to Him, what should our state be? Let us reflect on our position seriously. Do we fear God? Why do we not fear Him like they do? How can we bring ourselves to be like them? What are the incentives for fearing Him? What are the signs of this fear of God?

There are many questions that can be posed, and we will try to answer a few so that we are better able to follow the example and the model of the Prophet (s) and his Holy Household (a), as God has commanded us. *"There is certainly a good exemplar for you in the Apostle of God—for those who look forward to God and the Last Day, and remember God much."*[3]

GOD'S CLOSEST CREATIONS

Why do we not reach the level of fear of God that these divine personalities had reached, despite the fact that we are sinful and deviant, and they are immaculate and perfect? Should we not be more fearful because of our sin, disobedience, and deviance? Yet we go about our lives in this world as if we have no reason to fear God and the hereafter.

This all goes back to our knowledge of God. Whenever an individual becomes more knowledgeable of God, His Majesty, His Might, His Power, His Honor, and all of His boundless attributes, he will grow more and more fearful of

---

[3] The Holy Quran. Chapter 3 [Arabic: *Al-Ahzab*]. Verse 21.

God. God states this in the Quran, when He says, *"Only those of God's servants having knowledge fear Him."*[4] This was emphasized in the narrations of the Household of the Prophet (s). It is narrated that the Prophet (s) said, *"whoever was more knowledgeable of God was more fearful of God."*[5] It is also narrated that Imam Baqir (a) (or Imam Sadiq (a) in some manuscripts) related the following about the wisdom of the family of Prophet David, *"Oh son of Adam! Your heart has become [cold], as you have grown forgetful of God's Majesty. If you were knowledgeable of God and aware of His Majesty, you would remain fearful of Him...."*[6] And there are many more narrations illustrating the same concept.

This is a very natural relationship and we see it in our personal lives. If we lived under the rule of a tyrannical governor, we would see that the closest people to him are the most fearful of him, and will take any opportunity to please him. As for those who live far away from the tyrant's presence and do not know about his tyranny, they will not necessarily fear him in the same way. The same analogy can be applied to our fear of God.

Yet some may still pose the following argument. "If these righteous servants are so knowledgeable of God, they must know of His wisdom, mercy, and justice. So they will not fear him like a tyrannical king, but they will feel safety in his mercy and justice."

---

[4] The Holy Quran. Chapter 35 [Arabic: *Fatir*]. Verse 28.
[5] Al-Rishahri, *Mizan Al-Hikma*. 3:1888. Citing: Al-Majlisi, *Bihar Al-Anwar*, 67:393.
[6] Ibid. 1:835.

Those who are closest to God will fear Him because of a sense of shortcoming. They will fear that they have not fulfilled their duty of worship. They will know that they have not and will never be able to repay even the most minute of God's blessings. They know that every time they thank him, they have done so through the means of one of his blessings for which they must thank Him. Thankfulness itself is a blessing for which we must be thankful. The righteous will see that they are incapable of fulfilling their duty of worship towards God. This feeling of shortcoming will create a sense of fear in their hearts. This helps us understand the great deal of supplications that have been narrated to us from our Immaculate Imams (a), where they speak of shortcomings and guilt. It is not a feeling of guilt that we feel because of our sins. Rather, they feel guilt because they know that they are not able to fulfill this duty to God.

So if our Great Prophet Muhammad (s) – and he is certainly the best of creation – and his Holy Household (a) live in this state of fear, balanced with the hope for God's Mercy, what should our state and our position towards God be?

FEARING GOD

If being fearful of God is so important, how can we become fearful of God?

Knowledge of God

As we said, knowledge of God is the primary factor for fear of Him. Therefore, we must work tirelessly to gain knowledge of Him. The more we know of Him, the more fearful we will become of Him. *"Only those of God's servants having knowledge fear Him."*[7]

Reflecting on the Hereafter

Of the things that help us become fearful of God is reflection on death and the hereafter. Let us reflect on the horrors that we will see from the day our soul departs our bodies to the time of reckoning. Let us reflect on the punishments that have been prepared for the deviant and the disobedient. Let us reflect on the consequences of our actions. If every individual puts a side a few moments of his day to reflect on these things, he will no doubt begin to fear God. This is related in one narration of Imam Sadiq (a) as he speaks of the wisdom of the family of Prophet David (a):

> *Oh son of Adam! How do you speak of guidance when you are incapable of waking up to [the reality of] death. Oh son of Adam! Your heart has become [cold], as you have grown forgetful of God's Majesty. If you were knowledgeable of God and aware of His Majesty, you would remain fearful of Him and hopeful of His promises. Woe to you! How can you not remember your grave, and your loneliness in it?*[8]

The Commander of the Faithful (a) describes the need for us to be proactive when it comes to death and the hereafter. He says:

> *Hasten toward death in its pangs (by doing good acts) and be prepared for it before its approach, because the ultimate end is the Day of Judgement. This is enough preaching for*

---

[7] The Holy Quran. Chapter 35 [Arabic: *Fatir*]. Verse 28.

[8] Al-Majlisi, *'Ain Al-Hayat*, 1:423. Citing: Al-Tusi, Al-Amali, 203, Tr. 27.

one who understands and enough of a lesson for one who does not know.

What idea do you have, before reaching that end, of the narrowness of grave, the hardship of loneliness, fear of the passage towards the next world, the pangs of fear, the shifting of ribs here and there (due to narrowing of the grave), the deafness of ears, the darkness of the grave, fear of the promised punishment, the closing of the receptacle of the grave and the laying of stones?[9]

These are all horrors of the grave, and everything that comes after is much, much more. Reading such narrations and similar verses from the Quran reinforces the fear of God.

Realizing God's Oversight

Realization of God's oversight over us plays a role in strengthening our feeling of fear of God. When we reflect on our lives in this world and realize that there is someone who is overseeing all of our actions and keeping track of all of our sins, we will become wary of disobedience. We will be fearful when we realize that God's knowledge is all-encompassing and that he will punish deviance. Many of us observe the laws because they feel that they are under surveillance and will be punished if they break the law. When a state is weakened and law enforcement becomes feeble, we will find that many people will no longer respect the law. They will feel safe to break the law because they see that the state cannot enforce its laws.

---

[9] Al-Radi, *Nahj Al-Balagha*, 2:131, Sermon 190.

But God Almighty is never weakened, and His knowledge is
All-Encompassing. The narrations emphasize that we must
live in a state of realization of God's oversight. We must
observe his commands in public and in private, as He is always watching. We may not commit sin in public because
we fear our peers. We fear for our social status. We fear the
law. Not because we fear God. A person who is fearful of
God will obey him in public and in private. It is narrated
that the Prophet (s) said, "*[fear] God as if you see Him. [Know
that although] you do not see Him, He surely sees you.*"[10]

The narration emphasizes the importance of fearing God as
if we see him. Who of us dares to break the law when we
are in the presence of the police? If an individual has blinded his eyes from seeing God, he must know that God does
see him. "*[God] knows whatever there is in land and sea. No leaf
falls without His knowing it, nor is there a grain in the darkness of
the earth, nor anything fresh or withered but it is in a manifest
Book.*"[11]

How audacious are we to act with awareness of our community and our peers, but in heedlessness of God? It is narrated that Imam Sadiq (a) said:

> *Fear God as if you see Him. If you do not see Him, know
> that He sees you. If you think that He does not see you, you
> have disbelieved. If you know that He sees you, but you
> have committed sins, hiding them from the people, and open-*

10 Al-Rishahri, *Mizan Al-Hikma*, 1:825. Citing: Al-Majlisi, *Bihar Al-Anwar*, 67:7.
11 The Holy Quran. Chapter 6 [The Cattle; Arabic: *Al-An'am*]. Verse 59.

ly doing them before God, you have considered Him as the lesser [in significance] of all who may look unto you.[12]

The Benefits of Fearfulness

Fearfulness of God has many important rewards. Some of them are rewards that concern this worldly life, while others concern the hereafter.

Distance from Sin

One of the most important rewards of fearfulness of God is distance from sin. For the fearful, these sins are like pieces of trash that cling to the body if committed. Who would want to sit with himself, let alone others, if he knows that he is covered in dirt and reeks of rubbish? Sins form a layer of dirt over the soul that reeks stronger than any material impurity. Fear deters you from these impurities. The Commander of the Faithful (a) said, *"fear is the prison of the self away from sin, and its deterrence away from disobedience."*[13]

Knowledge

Fear of God is one of the paths to knowledge – not the knowledge that can be attained through study and observation, but the type of knowledge that God communicates directly to the believers and guides them to His path through. This type of knowledge only comes through obedience of God and fear of Him. This knowledge gives the individual who acquires it many abilities. It is the knowledge that allowed the righteous servant of God to bring the

---

[12] Al-Rishahri, *Mizan Al-Hikma*, 1:824. Citing: Al-Majlisi, *Bihar Al-Anwar*, 67:355.

[13] Ibid. 1:828.

throne of Bilqees, Queen of Sheba, to Prophet Solomon (a) in less than the blink of an eye.[14] This knowledge is only given to those who fear God, so that they only use it for what pleasures Him.

In reality, this type of knowledge is a knowledge without ignorance. It is narrated that the Prophet (s) said, "*if you were to fear God the rightful fear due to Him, you would be granted the knowledge that has no ignorance alongside it. If you knew God the rightful knowledge that is due to Him, the mountains would be moved by your prayers.*"[15]

Prestige in the Eyes of Others

One of the effects of the fear of God is that God grants his fearful servant a high prestige in the eyes of others. It is said that Imam Sadiq (a) said to Mo'alla ibn Khonais, "*Oh Mo'alla, gain honor through God and God will grant you honor.*" Mo'alla asked, "how is that done, oh grandson of the Messenger (s)?" Imam Sadiq (a) replied, "*fear God, and [God will make] everything else fear you...*"[16]

It seems that fear of God is directly linked to fear of others for the individual who fears God. If a person fears God, God will make everything fear him. If a person does not fear God, God will fill his heart with fear of everything. It is narrated that the Prophet (s) said, "*whoever fears God, God will make everything fearful of him. Whoever does not fear God, God will make him fearful of everything.*"[17]

---

[14] See: The Holy Quran. Chapter 27 [The Ants; Arabic: *Al-Naml*]. Verse 40.

[15] Al-Rishahri, *Mizan Al-Hikma*, 1:828. Citing: Al-Hindi, *Kanz Al-A'mal*, 3:142.

[16] Ibid. 3:5240. Citing: Al-Majlisi, *Bihar Al-Anwar*, 68:48.

[17] Ibid. 1:829. Citing: Al-Majlisi, *Bihar Al-Anwar*, 67:289.

When a person becomes fearful of God, he will realize God's power and glory. Everything else will be nothing in his eyes. A person who knows God will see that nothing has any value in the face of God's majesty and might. When a person only fears God's power, he will not fear anything else. Whoever fills his heart with fear of God, he will not be able to fear anything but Him.

Safety from the Greater Fears

When we see the horrors of the Day of Judgment and we are unsure where we will spend our eternity – how great of a fear will that be? However, God has promised security in the hereafter to anyone who is fearful of Him in this world. It is narrated that he Prophet (s) said:

> *God in His Highness and Glory said: By My Honor and Majesty, I will not combine two fears for any of my servants, nor will I grant them two sanctuaries. If he did not fear me in his worldly life, I will make him fearful in the hereafter. If he was fearful of me in his worldly life, I will grant him safety in the hereafter.[18]*

Claiming the Two Gardens

One of the rewards of fearfulness of God is the prize of the two gardens, as God has promised in the holy verse: "*For him who stands in awe of his Lord will be two gardens.*"[19] This is why the Prophet (s) gives the following advice to Abathar Al-Ghafari:

> *Oh Abathar, God, the Honorable and Majestic, says: "I will not combine two fears for any of my servants, nor will I*

---

[18] Al-Majlisi, *Bihar Al-Anwar*, 67:379.
[19] The Holy Quran. Chapter 55 [The Merciful; Arabic: *Al-Rahman*]. Verse 46.

grant them two sanctuaries. If he did not fear me in his worldly life, I will make him fearful in the hereafter. If he was fearful of me in his worldly life, I will grant him safety in the hereafter." Oh Abathar, if a man had the deeds of seventy prophets, he would still look down upon [his own deeds] and fear that he would not be safe on the Day of Judgment. Oh Abathar, a servant will see his misdeeds on the Day of Judgment and say [to God] "surely I was fearful of You," so He would forgive him. Oh Abathar, a man would perform a good deed and rely on it, and then commit sin, and he would come to God [on the Day of Judgment] as one of the wretched. Another man would commit a sin and become terrified of it, and he would come to God on the Day of Judgment in safety. Oh Abathar, a servant may commit a sin and [God would grant him] paradise because of that sin [...]. That sin would always be in his mind; he would repent from it and escape it towards God until he enters paradise. Oh Abathar, the practically intelligent one is the person who convicts himself and works in preparation for what is to come after death. The feeble is the one who follows his [lowly] self and its desires and wishes from God [to fulfill his empty] wishes.[20]

---

[20] Al-Tusi, *Al-Amali*, 530.

BIBLIOGRAPHY

RELIGIOUS SCRIPTURE

The Holy Quran

OTHER SOURCES

Al-Amili, Muhammad ibn Al-Hassan. *Wasa'el Al-Shia*. Beirut: Daar Ihya Al-Torath Al-Arabi.

Al-Andalusi, Ahmad Ibn Abdrabbuh. *Al-'Uqd Al-Fareed*.

Al-Asbahani, Abi Na'eem. *Hulliyat Al-Awliya'*. 1988.

Al-Asfahani, Al-Hussain ibn Muhammad. *Mufradat Ghareeb Al-Quran*. Qum, 1983.

Al-Barqi, Ahmad ibn Muhammad. *Al-Mahasin*. Tehran: Daar Al-Kutub Al-Islamiya, 1950.

Al-Bukhari, Muhammad ibn Ismail. *Saheeh Bukhari*. Beirut: Daar Al-Fikr, 1981.

Al-Haidari, Kamal. *Al-Taqwa fee al-Quran*. Qum: Daar Al-Sadiqain, 2001.

—. *Al-Tarbiya Al-Roohiyya*. Qum: Daar Al-Sadiqain, 2000.

Al-Hakeem, Muhammad Baqir. *Thawrat Al-Hussain (a)*. Najaf, 2008.

Al-Harrani, Al-Hassan ibn Ali. *Tohaf Al-'Oqool*. Qum: Muasasat Al-Nashr Al-Islami, 1983.

Al-Hilli, Ahmad ibn Muhammad. *'Uddat Al-Da'ee*. Qum: Maktabat Al-Wijdani.

Al-Hindi, Ali Al-Muttaqi. *Kanz Al-'Amal.* Muasasat Al-Risala, 1989.

Al-Huwayzi, Abd Ali. *Noor Al-Thaqalayn.* Qum: Ismailian.

Al-Kulayni, Muhammad ibn Yaqoub. *Al-Kafi.* Tehran: Daar Al-Kutub Al-Islamiya, 1968.

Al-Majlisi, Muhammad Baqir. *'Ain Al-Hayat.* Qum: Muasasat Al-Nashr Al-Islami, 2000.

——. *Bihar Al-Anwar.* Beirut: Al-Wafaa, 1983.

Al-Mazandarani, Muhammad Salih. *Sharh Usool Al-Kafi.* Beirut: Daar Ihya Al-Torath Al-Arabi, 2000.

Al-Mufid, Muhammad ibn Muhammad. *Al-Amali.* Qum: Jama'at Al-Mudarriseen, 1982.

Al-Muqarram, Abdulrazzaq Al-Mousawi. *Maqtal Al-Hussain (a).* Qum: Daar Al-Thaqafa li Al-Tiba'a wa Al-Nashr, 1990.

Al-Naraqi, Muhammad Mahdi. *Jami' Al-Sa'adat.* Najaf: Al-Nu'man.

Al-Nuri, Mirza Hussain. *Mustadrak Al-Wasa'el.* Beirut: Mu'asasat Aal Al-Bayt li Ihya' Al-Torath.

Al-Qummi, Abdullah ibn Jaafar Al-Himyari. *Qurb Al-Isnad.* Beirut: Mu'asasat Aal Al-Bayt li Ihya' Al-Torath, 1993.

Al-Radi, Muhammad ibn Al-Hussain. *Al-Majazat Al-Nabawiyya.* Qum.

——. *Nahj Al-Balagha.* Beirut: Daar Al-Ma'rifa.

Al-Rishahri, Muhammad. *Mizan Al-Hikma.* Daar Al-Hadith, 1995.

Al-Saduq, Muhammad ibn Ali. *Al-'Itiqadat fee deen Al-Imamiyya.* Beirut: Daar Al-Mufid, 1993.

——. *Al-Khisal.* Qum: Jama'at Al-Mudarriseen, 1982.

——. *Ikmal al-Din.* Qum: Muasasat Al-Nashr Al-Islami, 1984.

——. *Ma'ani Al-Akhbar.* Qum: Muasasat Al-Nashr Al-Islami, 1942.

——. *Men La Yahduruhu Al-Faqih.* Qum: Jama'at Al-Mudarriseen.

Al-Shaeed Al-Awwal, Muhammad ibn Makki Al-Amili. *Al-Mazar.* Qum, 1989.

Al-Shirazi, Nasir Makarim. *Al-Amthal.*

Al-Tabarani, Suleiman ibn Ahmad. *Al-Mu'jam Al-Awsat.* Daar Al-Haramain, 1995.

Al-Tabari, Muhammad ibn Jareer. *Tareekh Al-Tabari.* Beirut, 1983.

Al-Tabatabaei, Muhammad Hussain. *Tafsir Al-Mizan.* Qum: Jama'at Al-Mudarriseen.

Al-Tabrasi, Ahmad ibn Ali. *Al-Ihtijaj.* Najaf: Al-Nu'man, 1966.

Al-Tabrasi, Ameen Al-Deen. *Mujamma' Al-Bayan.* Beirut: Al-A'lami, 1995.

Al-Tabrasi, Radi Al-Deen. *Makarim Al-Akhlaq.* Manshurat Al-Shareef Al-Radi, 1972.

Al-Tabrizi, Muhsin. *Tafseer Al-Muheet Al-'Atham wa Al-Bahr Al-Khidam.*

Al-Tusi, Muhammad ibn Al-Hassan. *Al-Amali.* Qum, 1993.

—. *Misbah Al-Mutahajjid.* Beirut: Fiqh Al-Shia, 1991.

Al-Wasiti, Kafi Al-Deen Al-Laithi. *'Uyoon Al-Hikam wa Al-Mawa'ez.* Qum: Daar Al-Hadith.

Ibn Abi Al-Hadeed Al-Mutazili. *Sharh Nahj Al-Balagha.* Beirut: Daar Ihya Al-Torath Al-Arabi, 1965.

Ibn Al-Sabbagh, Ali ibn Muhammad. *Al-Fusool Al-Muhimma fi Marifa Al-Aimma.* Qum: Daar Al-Hadith, 2001.

Ibn Babaweih, Al-Hassan. *Fiqh Al-Rida.* Mashhad, 1985.

Ibn Katheer, Ismail. *Al-Bidaya wal-Nihaya.* Beirut: Daar Ihya Al-Torath Al-Arabi, 1988.

Ibn Qawlawiya, Jaafar ibn Muhammad. *Kamil Al-Ziyarat.* Qum: Muasasat Al-Nashr Al-Islami, 1996.

Ibn Tawuus, Ali ibn Moussa. *Iqbal Al-A'mal.* 1980.

Imam Zain Al-Abideen (a). *Al-Saheefa Al-Sajjadiyya.* Qum: Muasasat Al-Nashr Al-Islami.

Misbah al-Shariah. Beirut: Al-A'lami. (Attributed to Imam al-Sadiq (a)).